M000304636

Your Unique Facilitator Style

Explore Your Special Gifts and Powers as a Facilitator, Therapist, Teacher, Coach, and Helper

AMY MINDELL

Columbus, Ohio

Your Unique Facilitator Style: Explore Your Special Gifts and Powers as a Facilitator, Therapist, Teacher, Coach, and Helper

Published by Gatekeeper Press
2167 Stringtown Rd, Suite 109
Columbus, OH 43123-2989
www.GatekeeperPress.com

Cover art by Amy Mindell
Back cover photo by Liubov Sazonovo

Library of Congress Control number: 2019932643

ISBN (paperback): 9781642375411
eISBN: 9781642375404

Printed in the United States of America

Other Books by Amy Mindell

Riding the Horse Backwards:
Process Work in Therapy and Practice
(with Arnold Mindell)

Metaskills: The Spiritual Art of Therapy

Alternative to Therapy:
A Creative Lecture Series on Process Work

Coma: A Healing Journey

The Dreaming Source of Creativity:
30 Creative and Magical Ways to Work on Yourself

Contents

PREFACE
Senso-ji Dreaming

I N THE SPRING of 2015, Arny and I gave a series of seminars
in Tokyo. On a rare day off, while Arny was catching up
on some work in our hotel room, I had a bit of time and
followed a desire to wander through the beautiful grounds of
the Senso-ji Temple. The oldest Shinto and Buddhist temple in
Tokyo, the Senso-ji lay adjacent to our hotel.

For some time, I had been pondering the next steps in
my creative work. During the previous 5 years, I had focused
primarily on the creation of an animated video series about

Worldwork (the large- and small-group application of Process-Oriented Psychology).[1] Now, I wondered if I should continue with my animation work or turn once again toward my writing and research. Perhaps the Senso-ji would offer some advice.

*   *   *

Arny and I were on the final leg of our 'round the world travels, after completing seminars in Bogota, London, Moscow, and now, Tokyo. The many experiences from our seminars over the past 5 weeks had become a bit blurred, due to jetlag. However, now, with a bit of time to relax, the events began to unfold more clearly in my mind. Image after image rushed back to me. I recalled the many deep experiences working with individuals on their personal processes, as well as on their development as facilitators and elders. I remembered some of the powerful group processes that emerged in each country, revolving around social and political events that pressed and rattled upon each of these regions of our planet. Issues arose such as the long civil war and (at that time) impending peace negotiations in Colombia, and the relationship between Russia and many other parts of the world. The processes were riveting and moved me deeply. The methods and concepts that Arny and I shared were taken in by the participants and then infused with the special feelings, thoughts, knowledge, experience, cultural nuances, and gifts of each person, group, and place. The seminar participants were passionate about understanding and finding ever deeper ways for people to work together to resolve inner conflicts and outer world tensions. I breathed deeply, thankful for the immense luck to meet so many wonderful people, witness many transformative processes and, of course, to be able to work together and experience it all, with Arny

*   *   *

For nearly a quarter of a decade, Arny and I have visited, taught, enjoyed, and learned a great deal from the people and land of Japan. Over these years, our seminars have taken place in the Japanese countryside, in various city centers, and most recently, in the old town of Tokyo. Whenever we are in Tokyo, we gravitate toward the Senso-ji Temple. It has always felt like a refuge for us; a place of rest, wonder, and spiritual healing.

On most evenings after our very full seminar days, we roamed through the beautiful grounds of the Senso-ji on our way to a local restaurant. The environment around the temple is filled with quaint pebbled alleyways, awe-inspiring golden pagodas, brightly lit lanterns, and the stunning and illuminated black, gold, and red temples. Passing through the temple gates, we often found ourselves gazing at the giant, watchful gargoyles, standing guard and looking intently down upon us.

Our evening path always wound through the many stalls and storefronts filled with souvenirs, clothing, and toys. We passed by nearby streets lined with sushi-go-rounds, traditional Japanese restaurants, pharmacies, clothing stores, and even McDonald's. Walking back home one evening, I gasped as our eyes caught sight of the full moon shining brightly above the main temple's elegantly sweeping roof.

*   *   *

On this particularly warm springtime afternoon in May of 2015, the pathways through and around the Senso-ji swelled with local and international visitors. It was Golden Week, a traditional holiday of festivities, celebration, and prayer. Adults and playful children filled the grounds, while the smell of incense infused the air. Visitors placed aromatic incense sticks in sand altars, brushed the scented smoke back onto their faces, and then bowed in prayer. Throngs of people squeezed into alleyways, perused the festival souvenir shops, and bought tasty delights from the colorful line of food stalls. Many sat on chairs or smooth rock "benches," eating snacks and sipping green tea, or simply meditating. Long lines formed, as visitors waited to ascend the stairs to the main temple. Upon reaching the top, they prayed, bowed, and threw coins into a large receptacle.

After walking around for some time, I sat down on one of the stone benches to rest and quietly take in the atmosphere. After a short while, I felt relaxed and a bit dreamy. While in this foggy state of mind, I noticed a slight sensation, as if something was pulling or drawing me toward it. I had the strong feeling that something important was trying to catch my attention. At that moment, I heard a faint, yet vaguely familiar sound. Listening more closely, I realized what it was. For a small offering, people shook metal containers that held labeled sticks. This ritual was used to consult the oracle and divine answers to important life questions. Eventually, one stick would emerge from the container with a written paper fortune wrapped around it.

The ritual and the sound of the sticks clanking on the sides of the metal container immediately drew me backwards in time. During one of our first trips to Japan, Arny and I visited Nara Park in the ancient city of Nara, the first capital of Japan. Somewhere in the middle of the park, we happened upon an age-old shrine which, luckily, had an English fortune-telling booth. It was there that Arny and I shook similar containers and discovered our fortunes. Mine read:

> *No matter how hard one tries,*
> *it is impossible to grasp the moon's reflection*
> *seen on the surface of a pond.*

That experience, and the message I received at that time, gave me the initial inspiration for writing my first book, *Metaskills: The Spiritual Art of Therapy*. My term *metaskills* refers to the feeling attitudes or qualities that infuse all the practical skills we learn, whether we are therapists, doctors, cooks, or artists. Metaskills bring our skills to life and make them most effective.

I realized that metaskills are, as my fortune suggested, like "the moon in the water." They are a reflection of our basic attitudes that cannot be held or easily grasped in the same way as our learned skills. Yet, they are as important and influential as any particular "methods" we use—perhaps even more so.

*   *   *

My awareness slowly returned to the people around me and especially to the hardness of the stone bench on which I was sitting! Then, I had a sudden realization: It was exactly 25 years since *Metaskills* had been published! And in that moment, I had the urge to begin writing again!

This time, I hoped to widen my studies of metaskills and write about the larger and more encompassing concept of the facilitator's overall style. I had researched and given classes on this theme for the past 15 years. I was continually passionate to explore how our deepest selves and unique natures create our special way of working with others. For me, our unique styles are the greatest gift that we have to give to those with whom we work. Participants in my classes ranged from beginning students of psychology, to long-time therapists, supervisors, and therapists-in-training, coaches, organizational and group facilitators, palliative caregivers, teachers, home-makers, and many others. As I awakened to this realization, I felt a longing to put my learning, insights, and discoveries into words.

*   *   *

There is a beautiful story about the origins of the Senso-ji Temple. It is an apt metaphor for the way in which our deepest and most unique selves bring our work to life and create our special styles.

The Senso-ji is dedicated to the Boddhisatva, Kannon, or Avalokitsvara. The legend goes, that in 628 ce, two fishermen were fishing in the Sumida River in Tokyo. Deep in the water, they discovered a statue of Kannon (also known as Quan Yin). Though they tried to return the statue to the river, it always returned to them. The chief of the village recognized the sacredness of the statue. He decided to remodel his house into a small temple, with the statue enshrined there, so that villagers could worship Kannon. In 645 ce, the first temple was founded.[2]

For me, in a way, our unique style is like a statue or deep spirit that is hidden beneath the water. We do not normally see it. Yet, if we use our awareness, we can "fish it out of the water," so to speak, and bring it more fully into awareness. The original "statue" may, at times, sink back down out of sight, especially when we are exhausted, burned out, or feel uninspired in our work. However, it is always there, influencing all that we do. Its appearance at any given moment may take on a variety of forms, just as the water is constantly changing shape, but it emanates from the same deep source. With greater awareness, it is possible to tap into this source again and again, and to feel more at home and creative in our work.

*   *   *

When I returned to the hotel after my experiences at the Senso-ji, I was excited to share my experiences with Arny, and he was excited about them, as well! I felt ready to embark on this new book and had the sense that the spirit of Kannon would somehow guide me.

As I drifted off to sleep, I remembered the evening when the moon caught my attention as it shone so brightly over the Senso-ji. It seemed to be speaking to me once again, as it did so many years ago in Nara Park. I felt it was telling me that, like the moon in the water, our basic nature and style as facilitators cannot be firmly held, yet they inspire all that we do. And it was in this moment that this present book was born.

Amy Mindell, March 2019

Thank Yous

THIS BOOK WOULD not be possible without the loving
support of my partner and husband, Arny Mindell, who
encouraged and helped me in every stage of the writing
of this manuscript. I'm deeply grateful to him for his constant
search and discoveries about the nature of human life and our
universe. His development of Process Oriented Psychology is
the ground upon which this entire book is based.

I am grateful to the Process Work Institute in Portland,

Oregon, USA, for hosting many of my classes on the facilitator's style and being an enriching space for Process Work training and community. I am thankful to the many students of psychology, organizational facilitators, counselors, teachers, coaches, health care givers, spiritual guides, meditation teachers and others who participated in my classes, experimented with new ideas, and explored their own unique styles of working. I am also grateful to many of my friends, clients, and colleagues, all of whom provided me with helpful feedback. Special thanks to Lily Vassiliou, Lena Aslanidou, Ruth Weyermann, Kara Wilde, and Rhea for their helpful discussions and interactions about many of the ideas in this book, as well as my siblings Laura Berman, and Andy and Elaine Kaplan, for insightful conversations about some of the material and its applications to other professions.

I want to extend a big thanks to the worldwide learning community of students and friends of Process Work around the world. You have continually inspired my writing and research in innumerable ways. My heartfelt appreciation goes to Chikako and Yukio Fujimi, the Japan Process Work Center, and many of our Japanese friends for inviting us to Japan and introducing us to the Senso-ji Temple.

Finally, I am thankful to Margaret Ryan for many helpful interactions about my writing and her gifted and skilled editing of this manuscript. And a big thanks to Linda Innes for her warm-hearted and detailed final editing of the book.

INTRODUCTION
Your Crooked Tree

O NE MORNING, AFTER a very intense windstorm on the
Oregon coast, Arny and I went outside to see how our
garden had fared. I was shocked to see that a plum
tree that I had planted, loved, and cared for over the last ten
years had almost split in half. One of its main branches had
nearly broken off from the rest of the tree. While it didn't crack
completely, this branch, which had previously reached upward

toward the sky, now lay in a nearly horizontal position. My heart sank. I burst into tears. Luckily, a stump on the ground had caught the branch's fall and stopped it from cracking off completely. It was now suspended about two feet off the ground. After much sadness, Arny reminded me that nature sometimes has a different path than the one we hope for with our everyday minds. He also reminded me that trees never really die; rather, they transform.

At about that time, I had been thinking a great deal about the facilitator's style and the many therapists and facilitators whom I have taught and supervised. Some feel that they work quite well with others. Yet, many have told me that they feel they are not quite up to the job. They have a gnawing feeling that they are inadequate, "cracked," or different in some way. Many said that they sometimes, or frequently, feel that they are often not able to fit into a collective standard of how they imagine they should act as a facilitator. In addition, innumerable social issues and pressures play a big role in this feeling of inadequacy.[3] I was surprised to find that all of these self-perceptions applied not only to students-in-training but to many long-term practitioners, as well.

Keys to Your Greatest Gifts

The struggle to use your skills effectively, to meet certain standards, and to emulate a particular style is natural and can be very important. However, like my plum tree, nature bends, cracks, shapes, and forms each of us in utterly unique ways that do not always go along with a particular model. We are all just a little—or a *lot*—different, weird, bent, or unusual! There is just something about each of us that cannot be contained, put into a set category, or standardized.

Throughout my teaching and studies, I began to realize

that, paradoxically, it is just *within* our "crooked" nature that we can find the keys to our greatest gifts as a facilitator. It is just in our unusual qualities that we can find the seeds of each of our unique natures and the very special and individual way of working. As we become more aware of our unique natures and gifts, that awareness illuminates our skills and makes our work most effective. Our special natures transform and broaden all that we do and develop our special kinds of artistry.

The Story of the Crooked Tree

The struggle between feeling "inadequate" or cracked and outer standards reminds me of a wonderful story told to his children by the distinctive, unique, gravelly-voiced singer-songwriter Tom Waits. The story is called "The Crooked Tree."[4] Waits says that there was a moment when his children started to realize that he was different from other fathers. They wondered why he didn't have an ordinary job, like other dads do! He proceeded to tell them a story about a crooked tree and a straight tree that grew up together. The story goes something like this.

> Once, there were two trees: a straight tree and a crooked tree, that grew up together in a forest. The straight tree was very proud because it was handsome and tall. It made fun of the way the crooked tree was so bent. The straight tree was sure that no one would want to set eyes on the crooked tree!

> "Look at me ... I'm tall, and I'm straight, and I'm handsome. Look at you ... you're all crooked and bent over. No one wants to look at you."

One day, loggers came to their forest and decided to cut down only the straight trees. Waits said, "So the loggers turned all the straight trees into lumber and toothpicks and paper. And the crooked tree is still there, growing stronger and stranger every day."[5]

In this book, I hope to show you that the unique and "crooked" aspects of your nature contain the seeds of your greatest gifts as a facilitator.

And by the way, now, many months after that windstorm on the Oregon coast, my plum tree is growing and blooming more abundantly and beautifully every day!

PART I

The Nature of
Your Secret Power

*Like nature's boundless diversity of flowers, plants, trees,
leaves, insects, and animals, each of us is utterly unique.
Join me in a journey to explore your inimitable nature
and the way it creates your special facilitator style.*

CHAPTER 1

The Nature of this Book and Why I Had to Write It

*The meaning of life is to find your gift,
and the purpose of life is to give it away.*[6]

—Pablo Picasso, Spanish painter, sculptor,
and stage designer

THIS BOOK IS about exploring your unique style as a facilitator, therapist, coach, organizational consultant, teacher, or other type of helper. Whether you are a student-in-training or a long-time practitioner, this book will help you explore the special style that infuses your work and makes it most effective. Throughout the book, you will find yourself on a journey to get to know yourself better as a facilitator, and actually to know yourself better, as a whole.

After many years of teaching, supervising, and working with therapists and facilitators from around the world, it has become apparent to me that, although the skills and methods you learn are indispensable, it is the utterly unique way you bring your work to life that makes your work most effective. There is just something a little (or a lot) different about you and the way you use all you have learned. This uniqueness brings your work to life and is one of the central reasons that people are attracted to work with you, or continue to work with you, over time.

Of course, modeling what you do as a facilitator after others (e.g. mentors, teachers, icons in your field), or striving to match your performance to standards and norms of your particular profession can be an essential phase of facilitator development. Sometimes it is simply important to learn and practice more, in order to facilitate effectively, and to meet and pass certain requirements! Yet, without greater focus on your unique style, you might marginalize precisely those special qualities that will bring your tools to life in your own individual and most effective way.

One of the greatest paradoxes about your individual style is that, although it is basic to your nature, you're probably not quite aware of it. The style that exudes from you is like the invisible air you breathe. It has always been in the background, moving and influencing all you do. Therefore, it is not something to learn, but rather, something to remember.

Without greater awareness of the way your style influences your work, you will tend to lose energy, feel bored, or have the gnawing feeling that something essential is missing. You may lose track of the passion that first inspired you to do the work you do, and makes it meaningful and compelling. For no other reason, you'll want to read this book to avoid burning out and continue to love what you do.

When you are in tune with your own special way of working, you will have a greater sense of ease in your work and have the feeling of being "at home" in all that you do. Your skills will flow more effectively and you will feel more creative. You will sense the basic forces that *animate* your work and how even the most *unusual* or *quirky* parts of you, as well as your biggest learning difficulties, are the seeds of your special kind of artistry. In any case, you will never get around your unique style. It is, thank goodness, an irrepressible power!

We'll look at questions such as:

- What do you fall back on when you lose track of your skills, when you are tired or burnt out, or when you feel that your work has lost its meaning?

- In what way are you just a little, or a lot, different than others?

- How does your unique style support or inhibit your learning and use of skills?

- What are the basic components of your special style?

- How does your special way of working make your work most effective?

- In what way has your basic style accompanied you throughout life? In other words, how is it a mythic aspect of who you are?

And much more.

Your Unique Style Dance

I must confess that while writing this book, a critical inner voice kept making comments in my head that made me a little nervous! This inner critic said I should be able to give you a concise and simple description of your unique style in just *one sentence* that you could easily grasp and use immediately! I really wanted to do that!

However, I had to admit that the truth is much more interesting. My studies have shown that our styles are more complex and richer than any one simple answer could possibly encompass. In fact, far from being a static "thing," each person's inimitable style is a special blend of qualities, colors, dimensions, and what I call *substyles*, that *together* form a unique way of working. Together, these attributes form a kind of mythic dance that flows through each person's  work. In other words, each of our styles is a *process*, rather than being a fixed and static *thing*.

That dance or flow can't quite be expressed in words, even though it exudes from all we do. However, after exploring various facets of your style throughout the book, in the final section, you will have a chance to gather them all together and sense the larger, ineffable flow that moves and guides you.

My goal is to help you discover the beauty and complexity of your special way of working—the magic that makes your work most artistic and effective—and how this brings your skills to life in your own inimitable way. Ultimately, I hope you'll discover not only more about your style, but more about yourself as a whole.

Who I Am and Why I Had to Write This Book

For over 30 years, I have worked as a process-oriented therapist (Process Oriented Psychology, or Process Work), teacher, supervisor, and facilitator and have given seminars with my partner and husband, Arny Mindell, the founder of Process Work, all around the world. Arny's theoretical and practical discoveries, inspiration, and passion are behind each page of this book. Our process work seminars, conflict resolution facilitation, and organizational consulting have led us from Bogota to London, from Mumbai to Tokyo, from Moscow to Nairobi, and many other countries. My own journey to discover and embody my own style over these many years has been one of the most challenging, magical, and exciting parts of my self-discovery as a practitioner, and as a person!

In my first book, which I published in 1995, I described my discovery of the concept of *Metaskills*. This concept, as I mentioned in the Preface, is intimately linked with this current book. In that earlier book, I spoke about the *feeling* attitudes or qualities—which I called *Metaskills*—that bring the therapist or facilitator's skills to life and make them most effective. I referred to metaskills as the *"spiritual art of therapy."* I named some of the metaskills that go hand-in-hand with a Taoist- or process-oriented approach to facilitation, such as scientific and shamanic perspectives, a beginner's mind, and a capacity for movement and stillness, compassion, and fluidity.

Now, many years after publishing *Metaskills*, I realize that this present work is a natural next step. The facilitator's *unique style* is a more encompassing concept that includes all of your metaskills within it. In other words, your metaskills arise, flow out of, and are the central feeling qualities that make up your unique style. The present book takes the ideas in my *Metaskill* book further and shows how my thinking has evolved through classes, experimentation, and study.

In 2002, I published my second book, *Alternative to Therapy*, which focused on supervision ideas and methods and the concept of *process* in therapy. Some of my earliest ideas and exercises about the facilitator's style can be found in that book.

In my book *The Dreaming Source of Creativity* (2005), I focused mainly upon the way creativity is continually available by noticing how (what Arny calls) our *"dreaming process"* arises in the day or night and can lead toward continual creative expression. This present book is also an extension of this idea, showing that facilitators have an endless source of potential creativity within them.

My background as a dancer, singer–songwriter and artist have also compelled me to discover the unique self-expression of each facilitator, and the way in which each uses her or his tools creatively.

Over the past 15 years, I have avidly researched and studied the learning process and unique style of therapists and facilitators of all kinds. I have learned a great deal from the supervision seminars we have given in many countries, as well as the many classes I have given on the facilitator's style at the Process Work Institute in Portland, Oregon.

I have been fascinated by the learning process that facilitators embark on, and simultaneously, anguished by troubles that sometimes arise when trying to learn and apply skills. Though I myself have been practicing for a long time, I wonder why it is that I sometimes feel unable to use what I know. I have often felt "different," as if the way I understand and do things just doesn't fit in with the way "others" work. I have seen similar struggles in my student supervisees and even in long-time therapists. This struggle involves a tension between the use of skills and how those skills dovetail or conflict with a person's individual style. Of course, sometimes it's just important to buckle down, study, and practice some more. But when that isn't enough, I sensed there was a greater mystery that needed to be unfolded. This quest became a driving force behind my research and my constant desire to illuminate the unique qualities of each individual.

I feel it would be a great loss if the special qualities and gifts a facilitator has for her or his work were left uncovered. I hope this book can help nurture those qualities so they can blossom more fully in our lives and in our work with others.

What Is Process Work?

In order to understand the earth, from which the ideas in this book arise, let me tell you a little bit about Process Work.

In the 1970s and 80s, Arny began developing Process Work while living in Zurich, Switzerland. Process Work is a multi-leveled and multifaceted approach to working with individuals, couples, and groups. It is based on following the flow of nature. Like the ancient Chinese Taoists who studied and adapted to the constant changes of nature, Arny realized that we humans are also in the midst of constant change, though we often don't realize it. In fact, we tend to give static names or labels to our experiences. However, these static names are like freeze-frame pictures of a flowing river or *process*. Instead, we can follow that flow by becoming aware of the continual arising of signals and information, both inside of us and in the experiences of those with whom we work.

Arny discovered that if we follow and unfold our experiences with awareness, we can discover that *even in the most difficult experiences* such as troublesome body symptoms or relationship difficulties, there is *a great deal of wisdom and meaning.* This perspective of the treasure to be found in the difficulty might go against our logical way of thinking. However, it is a magical key to discovering that treasure of new solutions and information for ourselves and for those with whom we work.

In the early stages of developing Process Work, these central concepts were applied to such areas as dream and body work, relationship work, working with people in coma or near death conditions, extreme states, and movement work. And in succeeding years, many more applications were developed, including the use of Process Work to foster creativity and what Arny termed *Worldwork* (working with small and large groups, organizations, city forums, and in political contexts).

In essence, Process Work can be understood as a form of therapy or facilitation. But ultimately, it is much more than that; it is an *awareness practice* that focuses on what is arising in a given moment and following its unique flow. When we apply this idea to the facilitator's style, we find that it is just in the flow of our experiences that we discover the keys to our most unique gifts.

Deep Democracy and Substyles

A central idea in Process Work that is crucial to understanding the facilitator's unique style is Arny's concept of *Deep Democracy*. This term has to do with valuing *all of the dimensions* of our experience, both inside of ourselves and with those individuals or groups with whom we work. Those dimensions include *consensus reality*—that is, the ordinary reality about which people agree—deeper and more *dreamlike experiences*, and the realm of the *most subtle and deepest essence* in the background of all of our experiences.

To feel well in ordinary life, and to resolve personal and collective problems, we need to be aware of all of these dimensions. In the same way, facilitators need access to all dimensions within themselves in order to be fully present and in touch with their own styles. You will see in Part III that each of us has a number of *substyles* that arise from each of these dimensions.

The Design of the Book

While writing this book, I often felt that I should write it in a "normal" or "standard" way. To me, this meant that it should be very linear, serious, to the point, and full of important information! Although I appreciate that way of writing and it is an important part of me, my process of writing did not always go in that direction. After much sweat and hard work, it finally dawned on me that, since the book is about the facilitator's *unique style*, I should model my own style while writing!

Therefore, I allowed myself to flow through the many aspects and qualities of my own nature; sometimes I write in a linear way and at other times in a more nonlinear and unpredictable fashion. Some sections are more didactic and straightforward, while others more lyrical or dreamy. I use many images and metaphors to help convey the powerful, yet,

at times, illusive concept of *style*. My artistic nature appears in most of the artwork in the book (except where indicated) including some of my newest "flower art" creations,[7] as well as drawings, photos, and a puppet. Sometimes I interrupt the linear progression of chapters to give you an exercise that I feel will help you understand what I am speaking about in a more visceral way. These can be done alone or in a classroom situation. Interspersed throughout the book, you will find short vignettes and stories that spontaneously arose in connection with particular ideas that inspired me. I use many different metaphors to give you numerous images and words to describe your very unique nature and style as a facilitator.

I want to encourage you to follow your own flow and style as you read the book. Proceed in a linear way from chapter to chapter or move about randomly and spontaneously, as you feel pulled to certain areas that seem especially interesting to you. I tried to keep each chapter short, so you can enjoy bite-sized pieces whenever the need arises!

Please note that for ease, I often speak to you, the reader, as a therapist or facilitator. However, please know that I am speaking equally to facilitators of individuals or groups, and to coaches, social workers, spiritual guides, medical helpers, teachers, organizational consultants, and anyone in the helping professions. You can also apply the basic concepts and practices in the book to such things as public speaking, and to work in other areas, such as civic leadership, legal practice, and other professions. Similarly, while I often use the term *client* for the person you are working with, please adapt and interject other terms that suit your particular situation, such as *coachee, student, group, organization, patient* and so on.

Parts of the Book and Notes about the Exercises

Let me tell you a bit about the structure of the book and the exercises, and then we'll begin.

The book has two main streams. In the first stream, found in **Parts I and II**, I speak about the facilitator's style in *broad strokes*—that is, as an undifferentiated quality underlying all that you do. **Part I** focuses on the beauty of your unique style and how it is a secret power, of which you are not normally aware. **Part II** centers on how the unusual, weird, or crooked parts of you reveal crucial aspects of your special way of working. I also address the facilitator's learning process, how persistent learning difficulties are keys to your unique style, and the complex relationship between your style and the learning of specific skills.

In the second stream of the book, I differentiate your style into its various components and how these flow together to form your overall facilitator *dance*. In **Part III,** you will learn about your facilitator *substyles* and explore each of them through various exercises. **Part IV** gives you the opportunity to delve more deeply into what I call your "deep essence" substyle and its many facets. In **Part V,** we'll start to bring everything together. You will see how your overall facilitator style is *mythic* for you, meaning, patterned in your earliest dream or memory. In the exercises, you will get in touch with the flow of your substyles as you work. You'll sense how they animate and bring all that you do to life to create your seamless and unique facilitator dance.

Finally, in the **Conclusion,** I'll address how to bring your unique style more fully into your work and life.

The many exercises in the book will help you explore your style in action. Each one is derived from classes I have given over the years. Some of the exercises involve connecting with the earth, doing movement, making sounds, song, or masks, recalling special qualities you had in childhood, and many more. They are meant to help you know yourself better and experience the way your deep nature manifests in your work. I also provide numerous examples of the exercises from students and colleagues who have tried them in my classes or in private sessions with me. I especially hope that these examples will help you give yourself the freedom and space to try new ways of being and experimenting with your own style. I would advise you to take notes about your experience as you progress throughout the book.

Since the exercises come from my classes, they are sometimes written as if you are working together with a partner with whom you are practicing. However, if you are reading this book alone, you can *imagine* that you are working with someone else. If you happen to be studying this book with a friend or with a group, you can work with one another and share your learning. In this way, the book can be used alone or as a study guide for a class. The exercises may seem, at times, a bit too "programmed." Please adapt them to your own timing and particular situation and process. And please know that the point of the exercises is not to *succeed,* but rather, to explore your nature and unique way of working.

Finally, the way you use and integrate these experiences and ideas into your own work depends entirely on your specific situation with its various demands and constraints, the field in which you are working, its specific rules and restrictions, and the momentary field between you and your clients, students, or groups. Your own creativity and your deepest self will know how to adapt and bring this work most usefully into your life and work.

Ultimately, this book is about discovering and tapping into your most special power more fully. I hope you'll discover the way in which your unique style can renew your work; help you feel more at home, creative, and excited about what you do—and touch those with whom you work even more deeply.

CHAPTER 2

Your Secret Power

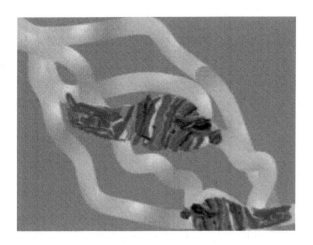

"When people like the path you walk and the style you walk in that path, they will start following you!" [8]

—Mehmet Murat ildan, Turkish playwright and novelist

A CCORDING TO THE dictionary, the word *style* is defined as the particular way in which something is done, created, or performed. In this book, *unique style* refers to your nature and way of working that are so basic to you that they emerge spontaneously, even when you don't intend it. Your nature is a special combination of many qualities that, together, create a subtle feeling or atmosphere you exude in your way of working. Like the "Tao that can't be said," it almost can't be spoken.

When you are lost, confused, unsure, or distracted, your style is a reorienting abode to return to, for clarity. When you are deeply connected to it, it feels like "home," as if you are coming back to an ancient part of yourself that has been forgotten. It is the place that you begin from and the place to which you always return.

Whether aware of it or not, your unique style is always in the background, guiding and inspiring you in your work. Yet, paradoxically, it's probably not well known to you! I want to tell you more about this; but first, let me tell you about one of my own experiences.

Style and Public Speaking

Some of the greatest learning I have had about my own "secret" style has occurred not only in the privacy of my individual client work, but at times, in the public eye, while teaching or lecturing. Let me tell you about one such experience that occurred some years ago.

One day, I was feeling quite nervous about a lecture that Arny and I were going to give to therapists and organizational facilitators about Process Work and conflict resolution. I had prepared parts of my lecture, which included a lot of didactic information. I hoped to convey many details about Process Work's theory and methodology.

For some reason, every time I attempted to go over my notes for this lecture, I became increasingly agitated. I found myself nervously shifting paragraphs around, trying to make the lecture flow in a more linear fashion. But, no matter how hard I tried, the notes just did not come together in a clear way. I was frustrated at first, and then, despairing.

At the same time, my attention was continually flooded by memories and images of *other* public speakers I had seen over the years. I'm shy to say this, because after so many years of public speaking, I think I should not be troubled by it anymore! However, even though I tried to blot out these images, I found myself trying to recall how each person behaved. How did they speak? Did they use written notes, or not? How did they begin their lecture? To my great embarrassment, I even found myself trying to remember what they wore! I urged myself to stay on track and go back to my notes and not be concerned with such trivial matters! But I had no luck.

Then, I was plagued by inner thoughts. "Who am *I* to do this? How could I possibly give a 'good' lecture?" A fleeting thought went through my head: "I should tell the organizers that I am sick and won't be able to come!" A flash of relief streamed through my body and, just as quickly, dissipated into thin air! As time passed, I felt as though a knot was being pulled tighter and tighter around my stomach and I could barely breathe!

When I told Arny what was happening, he empathized with my inner struggles. He also suggested that it might help to get in touch with what he calls the *Processmind*;[9] that is, the wisdom of the field around me. He thought that getting in touch with it might bring some helpful advice for my dilemma. (You'll have the chance to explore the *Processmind* in Chapter 19.)

One of the easiest ways to sense the Processmind is to temporarily let go of your ordinary mind, and allow yourself to be moved by the field around you. Then, as you move, notice what new experiences and insights emerge. So, I took a breath and tried to drop everything in my linear mind. This wasn't easy, because I was so agitated! However, after a couple of minutes, I was able to relax and let myself move about spontaneously. As I moved, I noticed that my upper back began to arch backwards and my arms opened outwards toward the side. At that moment, I felt that I needed to open up, and let something besides my everyday mind begin to guide me. I had the distinct sense that the lecture preparation was not simply *up to me*, but that I should let nature show me how to proceed.

Staying close to that feeling, I felt my heart opening wider. As my arms reached further outwards, I suddenly imagined embracing people who were attending the lecture. This surprised me, because I had been feeling shy and nervous about the people just a few minutes earlier! A soothing sensation flowed over me and I began to relax.

In that moment, a feeling I have had since I was a child washed over me. From an early age, I had an intense desire to reach out and connect with people. I longed to experience *everyone* as my family. I felt compelled to get in touch with something like an invisible *atmosphere* or *field* that connects us all. I had had this experience a few times as a young girl and it made me feel utterly at home in the world. I realized that this feeling was central to my nature; yet I often lose track of it, particularly when in stressful situations.

In that moment, I suddenly knew that I could not simply begin the lecture by speaking from my notes. Rather, I had to *feel the atmosphere,* first. I sensed that I also needed to speak personally and make a feeling connection with the audience. I realized that if I did these things, it would be much easier for me to flow with my linear lecture material. With that insight, I was able to go back to my notes and prepare my lecture in a more relaxed and fluid manner.

On the day of the lecture, I was a bit nervous, yet I was able to bring these insights to bear on the moment. I started out first sensing, then speaking about the atmosphere of the conference, and then, briefly about how I felt being there. I told them that I was moved by the many people gathered together, whom I imagined wanted to make a better world for their clients and for everyone, and I hoped that our lecture would support them in doing so. In that moment, I felt connected to the audience in a deep way, more at home in myself, and was able to give the rest of the lecture with a sense of clarity and meaning.

For me, this way of speaking and relating to the audience connected with something very basic within me. I also felt more able to flow between both my more feeling and sentient side and my linear and didactic nature.

After the lecture, I realized how important it is for all of us to connect to our own unique style and the ways that style wants to express itself in a given situation. This is not only a key to feeling well and using our skills in the best way possible, but also to deeply connecting with others. Each of us is needed in the world just as we are, with our *own* unique natures.

The Little Fish Story

Many of the people I know, I believe, would associate me with the way that I began the lecture I mention above. They would say that I am quite feeling, able to sense the field and connect with people, yet I can also be quite clear and didactic. However, I am not quite aware of these qualities in myself and how they flow from one to the other! That is, I know them . . . but somehow, do not!

Perhaps one of the biggest paradoxes about personal style is that most of us are not usually aware of or in touch with it! Even though these attributes are often the reason people are attracted to working with you, and especially why people will remain with you over long periods of time, you are often not fully aware of their presence! Your style, which reflects the fusion of these attributes, emanates from you and, I believe, is your greatest gift. However, it happens automatically and usually without your awareness. I sometimes playfully think of our style as our "default functions." It's the thing we naturally fall back on, again and again, even though we're often not conscious of it. In fact, most often, it is *other people* who can tell us about the special aspects of our unique ways of working. That is why I call it our *Secret Power*.

This paradox reminds me of a lovely Hindu story that Arny once told in one of his classes.

To say it simply, one day a little fish asked the Queen Fish, "What's this thing I heard about, called the sea?"

The Queen Fish said, "Well, the sea is the thing that is all around you."

And the little fish said, "Oh, I never noticed it before!"

You, I, and all of us, are like that little fish. We swim in the sea of our basic natures and styles, though we are frequently unaware of their presence. We don't realize the way the sea in which we swim propels and influences all that we do. We live and work in the midst of our special artistry and style, though we don't quite know it.

This reminds me of a session I once had with one of my long-time clients. She told me our sessions were often quite helpful for her. When I asked her what was helpful, she mentioned qualities I was not at all expecting! She said that she simply liked being in my office and wanted to be in my atmosphere, regardless of what I do! I was touched by what she said, but was secretly a bit insulted because I was trying so hard to be a "good" therapist and use my skills effectively! This brings to mind a quote by the great writer and poet, Maya Angelou. She said, "I've learned that people will forget what you said, people will forget what you did, but people will never forget how you made them feel."[10]

I want to stress that skills are extremely important! For me, the skills of Process Oriented Psychology are amazing, and even magical. They are crucial and are enormously important and transformative in my work with clients and groups. However, at the same time, the facilitator's unique style brings those skills to life and makes them most effective.

Throughout the book you will have the chance to explore many aspects of your style that, while utterly basic to your nature, you are probably not consciously aware of them.

On Not Feeling Close to Your Style

I want to add that it's also natural *not* to feel close to, aware of, or flowing with your unique style! If you are a musician, sometimes you have very inspired days. Then there are other days when you feel rather mundane, bored, ordinary, incapable, or frustrated. There are days, as a therapist, when I try hard to do what I've learned, but I can't seem to find the spark that brings my work to life. Yet, sometimes things seem to progress more fluidly and I find that I am flowing with my style.

Arny often says there is a natural process of remembering and forgetting. In fact, the great gift of losing awareness of your unique style is that you get so unhappy that you are *driven* to consciously seek it, once more! So, appreciate the ordinary you who feels messed up and distant from your special style, and also the beauty of searching and finding it again. And just to mix things up a bit, you'll learn, later on, that what seems like *just* the *"ordinary you"* is actually one of the many elements that make up your larger style and way of working!

Inner Questions

Before going further, take a few minutes to ponder some questions about your style. Don't think too much; rather, let the answers come spontaneously. Just catch the first responses that arise. You may not be able to answer them clearly at this moment, but take a few guesses and then, we'll go on.

- Why do you think people come to you, or would come to you, as a therapist, coach, teacher, facilitator, helper, or whatever you identify as doing? What would they say? Or, what have people already told you that they like about the way you work?

- Imagine being your own client, student, etc. What would you like about yourself? Why would you come to see *you*? Step over your shyness and say what is special or unique about yourself.

- Now, imagine stepping outside of yourself. Imagine being *the universe* looking down at you and say what you see that is very individual and special about you. You, as the universe, will know. Trust your intuitions.

- Make notes about your answers.

CHAPTER 3

The Ten Minute Break Experiment

B EFORE I BEGIN to teach a class, I often feel it is important
for the participants to have their own inner experience
of what I will be talking about. So, before I go further, I'd
like to give you a chance to try a short and fun inner experiment.
Afterwards, I will tell you what led me to creating this exercise

and how it applies to your unique style. I'll add another step to the exercise, at the end of the chapter, so please make sure to keep some notes about your experience. I will also refer back to this experience in Part V of the book.

The Ten-Minute Break Exercise

Imagine for a moment that you are having a really busy day. (For some, that may not be difficult to imagine!) Perhaps you have been consulting or working with people all day, studying, teaching, or whatever it is that you do.

Now, imagine that you suddenly get an *unexpected ten-minute break* in the middle of the day. During those ten minutes, you can do *anything* you would like to do that would make you *feel well*. This could be something that you *can't wait* to get off work to do, something that you *long for or are drawn towards*; it may be something you do *again and again* that you *love to do* and are often *compelled toward*. If many possibilities come to mind, choose the one that seems to grab you the most, just now.[11]

Now, I'd like you to actually *do that thing you are imagining in some way,* for a couple of minutes. That is, if it's possible to *actually* do it, please do. For example, if you would like to do yoga, go ahead and do a yoga posture for a couple of minutes. If you *can't actually do* the exact activity you are thinking of just now (like, climbing a mountain), then simply *imagine* doing it for a couple of minutes. As you do that activity, notice how it feels in your body. If you like, add some sounds or movements that go together with your experience. Take a few more minutes to allow yourself to sink more fully into that experience. As you do that, meditate on the quality of your experience and the feelings it brings to you. Sense how you need and enjoy this feeling and state of mind.

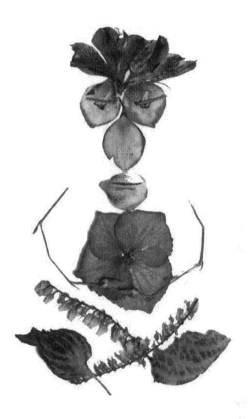

When I did this exercise in one of my classes, one participant said that she imagined staring at flowers in her yard. Others began to dance. One person laid back, relaxed, and found that this gave him a nonjudgmental inner feeling. He felt centered in his stomach and at ease. Someone else said that the experience brought her the feeling of just "being" and not working hard all the time. When I, myself, get a break in the day, I often go to my piano and begin to play music and sing. For me, this state is quite inward, spiritual, and has a dreamy quality about it that I intensely long for.

When you are ready, write a few notes in response to the following questions. There are many questions to ponder, and deep answers may arise over time. For now, just begin with jotting down the first glimmer that you sense, as a response.

1. What did you do? How did it make you feel? What is it about that experience that you long for? What type of body feeling did it bring to you? What is the deepest feeling that lies within this experience? Is this an altered state? That is, is it different from your ordinary state of consciousness? If you find it hard to describe this experience in ordinary words, try expressing it with a few lines of poetry.

2. Did you notice where your *focus* was, while you were doing that activity? For example, were you looking outward or inward? Did you sense where you were centered in your body (e.g. did you feel your center in your head, in your belly, etc.)?

3. Have you often longed for this experience/feeling? Are you aware of how this experience, or the feelings it evoked, has manifested in various forms throughout your life?

4. Finally, ponder: how often are you able to access this feeling inside of yourself while you are working with people? Maybe you do this a little, maybe a lot. Please make a note about this.

Note: If you are trying this experiment with other people, briefly share your experiences with one another. This is a quick way to get to know something deep and essential about one another.

This brief experiment may have shown you that there are things to which you are drawn in life that are absolutely central to your basic nature and sense of well-being. If this experience or the quality behind it comes back again and again in some form throughout your life, it is *mythic* for you—meaning a basic energy that has always moved and called to you in life. At the same time, it contains the seeds of an aspect of your unique facilitator style, which I'll be calling your *deep substyle,* later on in the book. At the end of this chapter you'll have the chance to explore it more deeply and apply it to your work. But before I say more, let me first tell you where the idea of the exercise originated.

The Inspiration for This Exercise

One day, a couple of years ago, while developing one of my classes on the facilitator's style, I was puzzled about which direction to take. The answer came to me after a supervision session I had with a therapist via telephone. When this woman called for the session, I was not quite ready and asked her to call me back in a couple of minutes. She agreed. However, after a few minutes passed, the phone did not ring again. I waited and waited.

Finally, about ten minutes later, the phone rang. I picked it up and asked her what took her so long to call me back. She said she was very sorry, but hadn't realized how late it was. I asked her what she was doing during those intervening minutes. She shyly said that she had started to play a musical instrument and had totally lost track of time.

She then said that she could use some help with her work as a therapist and also with some problems in her life. As she spoke, I recalled what she had said about those "ten minutes." I imagined that what she was doing during that time was somehow a key to what she needed. So, I asked her if she would play the instrument for me. She was surprised and said that my request was very unusual! She said she was a total beginner and had only begun to play this instrument recently. She was very shy to play it for anyone.

With a little encouragement, however, she picked up her instrument and did play a little bit. I was enchanted. Her music was beautiful and created a lovely mood and tone. When she put the instrument down, I asked her what it was like to play that music. She said that the feeling and sound of the music were very different from her ordinary way of being. Frequently, she felt quite worried and uptight. The music, however, brought her a different feeling. It was slow and meditative.

I then asked her to take some time and go a bit deeper into the experience and mood of that music. She played the music again and let it influence her feelings and body. She said she felt a deep part of herself rising up inside of her. She remarked that she somehow has always known this part of herself, but was ordinarily not in contact with it. She said the music created a meditative feeling and atmosphere that she loved. She remembered longing for this feeling, as a child, and at other times earlier in her life. It made her feel at home. However, in her current life, she did not experience it very much.

I encouraged her to take even more time to explore that feeling and experience; this time, without her instrument. She began to feel the qualities of that music in her body. As she did that, I asked her how she might use that deep feeling to help her deal with her problems in life and also in her work as a therapist. She said that she was often very rushed and anxious about her life and also, often felt the same way while working with her clients. She said this new musical feeling would help her to have a more meditative mood in her life, personally, and would remind her to slow down with her clients and notice more subtle signals in the client–therapist interaction. She imagined using this feeling with a particular client, and it was very helpful for her.

Moved by Mythic Forces

After the session with this woman, it dawned on me, that throughout life, each of us is strongly drawn toward certain experiences that we seek again and again, in some form. I began to ask many therapists, coaches, and group facilitators what moves them in life; that is, towards what are they naturally and passionately drawn? Some said they needed to seek a dark room. Others read a book. Some had to go into nature or take a walk.

The experience you just had when you took a "ten-minute break" is one such experience; it holds the keys to one of the central qualities behind your unique facilitator style.

If you are sometimes close to this experience while working, you will feel more at home in yourself. It will help you use your skills in your own way and will bring up new creativity that you might not have imagined before. Of course, you can't be close to this feeling all the time. However, if you are not close to it when you need it, you'll probably become bored, tired, spaced out, or confused while working. (Throughout the book, you'll have a chance to explore the many different qualities and forces that make up your special facilitator style.)

Shields of the Heart

Arny reminded me that these special experiences that we seek again and again in life are similar to Don Juan's (the figure in Carlos Castaneda's books) concept of *shields of the heart*[12]— those things that a warrior goes back to, again and again, for solace. A shield of the heart is something that is always there for you; something that you long for, and return to again and again.

I recall a therapist who told me that he had loved horseback riding as a child. He described the special feeling he would have while riding. He was very sentient and exquisitely attuned to the energies of the horse. He realized that he seeks this experience in many different forms and activities in his life. When he imagined applying this feeling quality to his clients, he first said that he ordinarily tries to be very related and in a kind of "uptime" mood. However, he realized that the horseback riding experience would create a deeper, more proprioceptive (body-feeling) experience of noticing and adjusting to the subtle changes and energies between him and his clients.

A school teacher told me that her shield of the heart was her love of sleeping! Her experience of "sleep" was closing her eyes and being very close to herself. When she imagined applying this to her classroom teaching, she felt that she would take time to go deeply inside of herself and, to her surprise, get in touch with a sense of lightness, freedom, and happiness! Though she was shy about it, she was excited to try to manifest this special shield more consciously in her teaching style.

Altered States

Often, we compartmentalize these activities and experiences toward which we are drawn. That is, we tend to do them only during breaks in the day or during special times or events; they are frequently not part of our lives and work, as a whole. A professional singer that I know says she feels quite passionate and ecstatic while singing. However, this passionate feeling only appears when she is performing. It is not at all a part of her daily life.

Why is this? One reason is that these experiences often involve altered states of consciousness. That is, they are different from your ordinary way of experiencing and expressing yourself. Because of this, you might be shy to bring the experience consciously into your life and work. That's fine, even natural. However, the essence of those experiences is basic to your nature and wants to influence and enrich the work that you do.

Taking the Exercise Further

I'd like to give you a chance to take the earlier experiment a bit further in order to sense how you might apply that experience to your own work with a particular client, student, or group. Please adapt this exercise to fit your particular situation, such as therapist and client, teacher and student, coach and coachee, group facilitator and organization, etc. You will also need a pen and paper to make notes. Afterwards, I'll give an example from one of my supervisees.

Recall the activity you did when you had a 10-minute break. Remember the feeling and state it evoked within you. Feel it once again in your body. If you like, add sounds, movements, or do anything else that helps you to access and vivify this experience a bit more. Notice how this experience affects the way you use your eyes, your focus, your posture. Sense, once again, what it is about that experience that really moves you and that you long for.

Continue to feel that experience and express it a bit stronger now, *in general* (that is, not necessarily associated with a particular activity) and imagine that you are some kind of real or imaginary figure or being, who is acting this way. As you do that, sense the *unique style* this figure and experience are suggesting for your work with people. How might you act/be? Imagine how you would use your posture, the way you would use your eyes, voice, etc.

When you are ready, imagine a particular client or group with which you work. Choose a client (or group) with whom you have trouble working, or any client (or group) who comes to mind. Then, imagine how you might use that style while working with her or him (or group). In your imagination, what would happen? How would you be different than you normally are? What effects might this have on the other person (group)?

Finally, consider and make notes about the following:

- How is this unique style experience similar to, or different from, your ordinary way of working?

- What did you learn about yourself as a therapist/ facilitator?

- Are you aware of how this experience/style has come up, or tried to come up, previously in your

work (consciously or unconsciously) and in your
life, at different times?

An Example

Here is an example of the exercise from one of my supervisees,
who is a therapist. This woman said if she had ten minutes free
during a busy day, she would lean back and be very quiet and
nonresponsive. She would not do anything for, or interact with,
others. She said she would be centered in her belly. She had an
image of this experience as a Buddha under a tree. She then
remembered that she has a Buddha figure in her office! She
loves this figure but didn't know why. She said the feeling of
this experience has appeared in many ways throughout her life,
particularly in her interest in, and love for, meditation. I was
impressed by the way we tend to surround ourselves with these
experiences, but often don't realize it!

When I asked her what style this experience would suggest
for her work, she said that she would just "be"; that is, she
wouldn't have to do much. She would just be who she was and
would stay very deep within herself. While sitting with her
clients, she would let impulses come through her and follow
them.

When I asked her to think of a particular client and imagine
using this style with that person, she chose a client who was
quite difficult for her. She said this client was frequently upset
and full of anxiety. She imagined what it would be like to sit
quietly and follow her impulses with this person. She imagined
herself saying to the client, "Be quiet for a moment, grow
roots, and try sitting quietly." She realized that she normally
gets pulled into an anxious state herself when she is with this
person, in her efforts to try to find a solution. But she sensed
that, when both she and the client were quiet, she would be able

to connect more fully with her own internal experiences and catch impulses that come, as to what to do. She told me, later on, that this exercise was a great way to do self-supervision! We'll return to this experience in Part V, where we'll explore how it is connected more fully to your long-term personal myth. In Chapter 17, you'll also have a chance to further explore, the way in which experiences that have drawn or compelled you since childhood, are central to your unique facilitator style. For now, let's turn to the next chapter, where I will sum up some of the salient points about your facilitator style. Then, in Part II, we'll begin to explore how the learning process supports or inhibits your individual style, and how imperfections are keys to your unique facilitator gifts.

CHAPTER 4

The Importance of Following Your Unique Nature: A Brief Summary

"You were born an original work of art. Stay original always."[13]

—Suzy Kassem, Egyptian and U.S. writer, poet, philosopher, and multifaceted artist

T HE LINEAR PART of my style is emerging once again. So, before turning to Part II, I'd like to sum up some of the salient features of the facilitator's unique style and add a couple more to the list. I'll speak more about some of these elements in the upcoming chapters.

A gift: Your unique style is a gift that you were given. You can't even take credit for it! It is simply there, part of your deepest self that wants to be known and used. It has been there since childhood, or depending on your belief, since before you were born.

Your secret power: Your most special qualities are often not quite known to you, even though you swim in them like the water surrounding a fish. So, your style is not something to learn, but something to remember. You continually grow into, forget, and then become aware of it again and again, throughout life. It is often others who can tell you about the special qualities of your style better than you can yourself.

The things that move you in life: You can discover an aspect of your unique style by noticing those activities in life that draw you, that move you, that you long for, and particularly those that come up again and again, that you go towards for a sense of solace or "home." These activities reveal a central aspect of your deepest style.

Your default function: Neither you nor I will ever get around your unique style. I sometimes call it your *default function*. That is, no matter what you have learned or how hard you try to change or adapt yourself to a given norm or standard, you will always revert back to the most unusual, unique, and inimitable you! Thank goodness! The artist Robert Henri said, "Don't worry about your originality. You could not get rid of it even if you wanted to."[14]

Your style is a crucial part of your teaching, yet you often

don't realize it: When you do therapy, or when you teach, coach, or facilitate a group or organization, your focus may be on one aspect of your work. However, you often don't realize that one of the most important things that you have to give and teach is your special nature and style.

Style as artist: Your unique style is like a painter's brush that breathes life and magic into your canvas. It is an abundant source of creativity. Learn all the skills you can; they are invaluable methods and guideposts for your work. But remember that it is your *special brushstroke* that brings those skills to life in your own inimitable way.

Congruence, feeling at home, and less burnout: When you are connected with your unique style, you will feel more at home. You will experience more congruence in all that you do, and you will have a greater sense of ease in your work. This congruence will help you continue to love what you do, instead of burn out from it. At the same time, when you are in touch with your style, you will also become a model—of a person who follows her or his unique nature—to your clients, colleagues or co-workers.

Mild chronic depression: If you are not in touch with your special way of working, you might develop what Arny calls a "mild chronic depression." That is, life and work are OK, but they are missing a certain spark. You may find that you get bored, tired, or even begin to dread your work. You might feel that you are losing connection with what moves you. When you are in touch with your style, it can bring back a sense of purpose and inspiration to all that you do.

Skills work best: If you are in contact with your unique self, your skills will become more fluid and you will use them most effectively.

Your best calling card: People come to you and/or will stay with you over long periods of time because of who you are:

your special style. In other words, you are your own best calling card! The most important tool you have for working with others is the unique way you work and move through life. Arny once said in one of his classes, "Learn linear skills, understand dream symbols, follow signals, etc., but remember the deepest feelings of who you are; it has an unteachable ability to help others."

An eternal guide: When you get confused in your work and the path becomes unclear, one of the most helpful things to do is to sink back into your unique style. It is a constant guide on which you can always rely.

Finding your rank: Therapists, facilitators, and teachers have a lot of rank or power in relation to their clients/students. This power needs to be used with great awareness. However, paradoxically, facilitators sometimes feel small, as though they have *low rank* in relation to their clients' problems or powers (whether they are working with an individual, group, or an organization). Some group facilitators, for example, feel overwhelmed when facing the tensions of group issues. Some therapists feel overwhelmed by the intensity and complexity of a given individual's life situation. When you, as a facilitator, are in contact with your unique style, it will help you gain the necessary sense of rank and centeredness to deal with difficult and challenging situations.

Style as a diversity issue: Living and being in touch with your unique style is not only important for your work with others, but it is also a social diversity issue. It is both a personal matter and also a cultural one. Why? No matter what we you do in life, there is a *mainstream* way of doing it and there is also *your unique way* of doing it. While it may be useful or important to adapt at times, it's equally important to appreciate and value your own unique style. Perhaps we need an entire culture or world change, to open up to and support the vast diversity, not only in the crucial realms of religion, race, gender, sexual orientation, health, and many other important social issues; but also, in a broad sense, the *diversity of styles* in facilitation, education, and many other areas, as well.

Learning difficulties and imperfections: The most insistent learning difficulties, and even your seeming imperfections, contain the seeds of your unique style of working. So, let's turn to Part II and begin to explore these fascinating connections!

Incomparable Style

A Short Vignette

W̶HEN I THINK *about the concept of unique style, my mind often turns toward musicians whose styles move me deeply. Let me wander for a brief moment, to tell you about one of them.*

Whenever I hear Joni Mitchell singing, whether I am at home, in a crowded bus, or sipping tea in a café, I fall into an altered state and totally forget where I am! I could be in Portland, Oregon, or Tokyo, Japan, in a crowded store, or in a restaurant eating dinner, and I instantly lose track of what is around me. I immediately know who is singing and playing, and an indescribable feeling of wellness washes over me.

Like many others of my generation, I grew up listening to Joni's records. I played them over and over again. Her music inspired me to believe in my own musical sensibility and helped me dive wholeheartedly into the piano, guitar, and dulcimer, as well as singing, painting, and poetry. When I listened to her records, I couldn't stop myself from singing along—stretching my vocal chords to their limits, as my voice slid helplessly from one end of a scale to another. All the while, I accompanied myself humbly on my instruments.

While there are many gifted singers and musicians that held my attention during my teens, it was Joni's incomparable style, the exquisite way she expressed herself in words and tones that moved me deeply. Her voice made me dream. Her songs inspired me to create my own imaginative stories, all the while buried in the confines of my little room. Whenever I was feeling down, I ran to her music for solace; a self-healing ritual I depended upon.

Although Joni drew from many musical styles in her songwriting, I instantly recognized that it was *her*. There was just something about her voice and style that said "Joni" to me—like a unique signature or brushstroke. I'm reminded of something that *New York Times* music critic Nate Chinen said about the great jazz musician and composer, Chick Corea. "He's one of the greatest Fender Rhodes pianists ever . . . his touch on that instrument is really distinctive. You know it's him within a note or two."[15]

In the same way, some might look at a painting, and immediately know that its colors and shapes were brought to life through the hands of Vincent van Gogh. Others might read powerful and poetic words and know that they were written by the poet, writer, and playwright, Maya Angelou. The very essence of each artist shines through each word, note, or color. It is inimitable and unforgettable.

Joni works with melody, rhythm, and chord progressions. She flows between varied musical styles, rich harmonies, and complex orchestration. Yet, the way she brings her feelings, poetry, chords, and melodies to life is utterly unique and incomparable.

In the same way, therapists, facilitators, coaches, teachers, and helpers of all kinds learn crucial skills for their craft and often take many years to digest and refine them. Those methods form the backbone of their work. However, no matter what you learn, and no matter how many years of training you have had, the artistry with which you use those methods, the *way* they come to life through you, is *utterly unique*; it is *your* unique signature, your inimitable style in all that you do. And I believe it is this *incomparable style,* recognizable from both close and far away, that is your greatest gift.

PART II

The Gifts of Imperfection: The Facilitator's Cracked Pot

CHAPTER 5

Introduction to Your Cracked Pot

*"There is a crack in everything.
That's how the light gets in"*[16]

—Leonard Cohen, from his song, "Anthem"

THERAPISTS, FACILITATORS, AND helpers of all kinds are like pots that hold the clients, organizations, and communities with which they work. Each pot is also filled with an abundance of learned skills and knowledge. Most "pots" that I know try to be perfect! That is, facilitators try to use the skills they have learned as best, or as perfectly, as possible!

However, even with the greatest effort, practice, and determination, cracks inevitably appear in your facilitator's "pot," whether you are a beginning or long-time practitioner. Sometimes, cracks appear in the persistent inability to learn or execute certain skills. At other times, there is just something about you that doesn't quite fit in, that is weird, unusual, different or special, that can't or doesn't use your tools and knowledge in the way you think you should. This can occur whether you are a new student or long-time practitioner.

If you are able to have an open-hearted attitude towards

your differentness, or your persistent "flaws," you will find that it is just in those "imperfections" or "cracks," that you can find a doorway into your most unique self and style. Daisetz Suzuki, a Japanese author of books on Zen Buddhism, suggests that an irregular curve is perfect in its imperfection.[17]

In other words, imperfection is, in a way, more beautiful, because it mirrors actual nature.

Highlighting the Cracks

In this section, I'd like to illuminate the *cracks* or *imperfections* in your pot in order to bring out the artistry and unique style within it. I am reminded of a Japanese pottery repair method I learned about some years ago called *Kintsukuroi* or *Kintsugi*. This method does not try to *hide* imperfections and cracks in a pot, but rather, brings them out *even more!* The pottery repair person fills the cracks with lacquer that has been dusted with gold, silver, or platinum powder.[18] The golden cracks then *illuminate* the history of the object, rather than trying to cover it over or disguise it. The resulting bowl is an even *more beautiful piece of art.*[19] The method of *Kintsugi* is akin to another Zen concept called *Wabi Sabi*, which has to do with embracing what is imperfect or flawed[20] as well as treasuring what is simple, aged, unpretentious, rustic, weathered, and impermanent.[21]

The idea of highlighting the "cracks" is mirrored in a basic tenet of Process Work. That is, within the disturbances, mistakes, or experiences that do not go along with our intentions, lay the seeds of rich information and potential solutions to our problems. As Leonard Cohen says in his song, "Anthem," it is just in the cracks that the light is able to shine through.

The Chapters

In the following chapters, you'll have the chance to explore various cracks in your facilitator pot and how these reveal aspects of your unique style. In Chapter 6, we'll begin by exploring cracks that arise during the learning process. In Chapter 7, you'll have the opportunity to explore how aspects of your style, which make you different, weird, or unusual, appear through one of the cracks. In Chapter 8, I'll carry the metaphor of the cracked pot further and actually help you to *create a crack* in your pot in order to *shed greater light* on your unique style! The last chapter, "Sculpture within the Stone," is even a bit *more* radical! There, you'll temporarily crack your pot *altogether,* discovering what is left and which aspect of your style appears!

Along the way, I provide experiential exercises. You can do them internally as a form of inner work, where, at certain points, you will *imagine* that you are working with a client (or student, coachee, etc.). You can also do the exercises with a learning partner who will lead you through the exercises and help you explore using your style, as well as help you practice by acting like one of your clients. Please take the liberty to adapt each exercise to your specific situation or type of work. That is, if you work as a therapist or coach, you can ask your learning partner to act like a client. If you are an organizational facilitator, you can ask your learning partner or partners to act like a group, and so on.

In this section, we will continue to explore your unique style in broad strokes. Then, in Part III, we'll begin to break down your unique style into some of its individual components or substyles. Let's begin, now, by looking at the learning process and how learning difficulties contain the seeds of your unique nature and facilitator style.

CHAPTER 6

Learning Difficulties as Gifts

The brush must draw by itself.
This cannot happen if one does not practice constantly.
But neither can it happen if one makes an effort[22].

—Alan Watts, British-U.S. philosopher

*O*NE OF THE *ways your unique style makes its presence known is, paradoxically, through persistent difficulties that arise either during the learning process or while working with others. These repetitive "cracks" are hidden keys to some of your greatest facilitator gifts. In this chapter, we'll begin by looking at the common tension that arises between learning specific skills of your chosen profession and your personal style. In the next chapter, you'll have a chance to take things further and explore one of your own persistent problems or "cracks" as a key to an important aspect of your facilitator style.*

The Dance between Skills and Personal Style

No matter what you try to learn in life, from the martial arts to mathematics, from coaching to therapy, or from football to playing a musical instrument, there is often tension between learning specific methods and your personal style. How do the methods or skills that you need to learn dovetail, or conflict, with your unique way of doing things? The convergence between skills and personal style can bring difficulties and challenges, as well as exquisite moments when one's skills and individual style meld together into a seamless flow.

For many years, I have been fascinated by this tension between skills and personal style. How can skills and style enhance and support one another more fully? As a teacher and supervisor of facilitators, I often find it challenging to teach practical methods while supporting each person's unique way of using them.

While helping students learn to use a core set of skills, I have frequently noticed that even after a lot of practice and study, some students are not able to use what they have learned. I was especially intrigued that this seemed to happen in moments when all problems were put aside, when it would be reasonable for students to be able to use their skills. I felt agonized for them, while also wanting to fulfill the goals of my job!

Of course, there are many reasons these problems might occur. At times, I just need to learn more about *how* to teach! At other times, it is simply natural to have some frustration while trying to learn something new. Maybe the student needs more time to study and practice. As Pablo Picasso once said, you need to first *"Learn the rules like a pro, so you can break them like an artist."* [23] Another possibility is that the student is just having a bad day. Maybe she or he simply gets uptight when tasked with demonstrating particular skills in front of me. I totally understand these problems and have experienced each of them many times, myself!

While all of this applies to students-in-training, Arny and I have also noticed that long-time practitioners whom we have supervised around the world often struggle with similar issues. Practitioners of all kinds feel embarrassed when they are blocked and unable to use or remember the skills they hold dear! While it's natural to lose connection with your skills when, for example, encountering tense situations, or when social issues emerge that trigger inner difficulties, there are other times when it would be reasonable for the facilitator to recall what she or he has learned. When this doesn't happen, it can feel quite distressing! All of these experiences led me to think there was a missing key to this dilemma.

Before going further, take a moment to remember a time when you wanted to learn something, but no matter how wonderful the teacher was, or how many times you tried to learn, you just couldn't get it. Perhaps the teacher wasn't very good, or you, the learner, didn't really want to learn! But let's say, hypothetically, that everyone was doing their best and that you were completely capable of learning. Think about one of these times in your life.

If you are a long-time practitioner, do you remember a time, or perhaps *many* times, when you just couldn't seem to use what you know; when something seemed to get in the way? Again, let's assume that conditions were such that it would be reasonable for you to remember and fluently use your skills. What can we learn, here? All these questions led me to realize there is a mystery about the learning process that I had not yet discovered.

A Gift Unrecognized

My greatest learning about all of this comes from something Arny came upon, many years ago, in one of his case supervision classes. I remember a particular therapist who presented a case situation about a client with whom he, the therapist, was having trouble. He asked Arny for suggestions how to understand and work further with that client. Arny gave him many suggestions, but the therapist stared back at Arny in a kind of blank way. Arny repeated himself and tried many new ideas, but received the same blank stare. The therapist said that the methods Arny was suggesting would probably be helpful, but for some reason, he was not able to pick up the suggestions. Why?

Arny then realized that if you are not able to grasp information, even when it would otherwise be reasonable to do so, it is an indication that *there is something else in the background that is trying to be known.* That is, something important is *blocking or stopping you* from receiving that information. In other words, *the problem is not simply to be overcome.* Rather, he said that behind a persistent learning difficulty lies *a gift that is not yet recognized;* a gift that wants to be known and used, before it will allow other learning to happen!

Let me say that again. One of the reasons that people *don't* learn something, even if they have tried many times and it would be reasonable that they could, is that there is a *gift in the background* that is blocking them from that learning. *This gift wants to be known*, and only when it is appreciated and used, will it open up to other ways of learning.[24]

After experimenting with this idea, I realized that, most importantly, *this gift contains seeds of your unique style*, and wants to be recognized and brought into your work. Only then, will it allow you to open up to other methods and skills! For example, if you are someone who has a lot of inner visions and intuitions, you might have trouble seeing the outer signals of your clients at times, because your inner wisdom wants to be known, first. In other words, it might block your *outer awareness*, until you first go *inside* and follow your inner wisdom.

In short, a persistent block in your learning or in your ability to use your tools is not simply a sign of your incompetence! Rather, it is trying to show you your unique way of doing things; that is, a part of your unique style is trying to emerge. All of this follows a basic Process Work tenet: it is just in the disturbances or things that bother you in life that you can find the seeds of new information and resolutions!

This reminds me of a woman who came to me to work on her problems as a teacher of psychology. She felt she should be like other teachers who are more extroverted, present, and cognitive while teaching. However, she said that whenever she would force herself to be more "out there," she would tend to forget entirely what she was trying to say. She felt blocked and unable to remember what she was talking about. This made her feel embarrassed and a failure.

Assuming her "inability" was trying to reveal an important part of her style, I encouraged her to literally *block* herself; that is, to stop herself from focusing outwardly and notice what else was happening. As she did that, she heard something inside of her say, "Follow your hands and feelings more. I won't let you do anything else." It turns out that this woman is an artist and had earlier been a body worker. She realized that her natural way of understanding the world is through art and touch. It occurred to her that in order to feel well, she would need to engage her classes in various kinds of creative art projects to understand the material in a creative and tactile manner. She would also need to follow her own body more, instead of pushing herself to relate outwardly to the class. When she imagined using this artistic and body-oriented style, she felt she would have more access to spontaneous insights that bubbled up inside of her. In so doing, this would also free her cognitive mind to emerge naturally.

In another instance, a therapist told me that she wanted to be very compassionate and feeling with her clients. She felt that empathy was very important but could not seem to produce the feeling she was looking for. This was very frustrating for her. When I asked her what she was doing instead, she said that she was always *thinking* about the content and structure of what was happening with her client. But she felt that this was getting in the way of being empathetic! In this case, I told this woman that perhaps she was much more analytical and didactic than she allowed herself to be. She said this was right and that she didn't think she *should be* so objective and distant, as a therapist! However, she loved to think and analyze things! I encouraged her to appreciate this part of herself even more. When she experimented with being more linear and didactic with her clients, she felt more at ease and this, in turn, freed up her other "empathetic" feelings and abilities, as well.

As you can see, the part of us that blocks our ability to learn is a very powerful force that cannot be easily bypassed. Yes, of course it can be very important to simply learn particular methods and practice again and again. But when that isn't enough, and learning problems persist, remember that that which is blocking you might be a gift; *an aspect of your unique style beckoning to be recognized and used.* It is a great power that you will not get around, thank goodness! It is core to who you are and your most unique way of working.

Perhaps it would help to think of all of this in terms of another basic Process Work idea. That is, if you try three times to do or learn something and you are unable to do it, there is another pathway that is trying to reveal itself to you.

Double Signals and Your Gifts

There is a very practical and important reason to notice hidden gifts behind learning difficulties and bring them more consciously into your work. If you are not aware of them, they will seep out of you, anyway! How? They will appear in your unconscious body signals, or what Arny has called *double signals.* Double signals are those gestures and motions you make that you are not identified with or aware of, in a given moment. For example, if the teacher who needs to follow her sense of art and touch does not follow those tendencies, she might *act like* she is listening to her students but *at the same* time *look down* from time to time and lose track of what she is doing. Or she might be overcome by a sense of fatigue which, when followed, would draw her inwards, in order to follow her hands and body sensations. Without awareness of the gifts trying to realize themselves, facilitators tend to become incongruent and unable to be fully present.

Education and Social Issues

Of course, the tension that sometimes arises between learned skills and personal style is not only a challenging problem for facilitators but is found in all forms of education, as well. Many people have had troubles in school and have been made to feel ashamed for their different ways of learning or understanding the world. Again, it can, of course, be important to adapt to a particular system or culture, at times. However, when the clash between mainstream styles of learning and other styles is not recognized or processed, it can become the source of great tension and agony.

I will never forget the painful story told to us by an Australian Aboriginal woman. When she was in elementary school, her teacher told her to stop "dreaming." The teacher told her to go into the corner, and then, the teacher promptly put a "dunce cap" on the young woman's head. This is so very, very painful and especially so, due to the fact that *Dreaming and Dreamtime* are central aspects of Aboriginal culture and spiritual beliefs.

Of course, this interplay between mainstream approaches and individual styles does not only occur in the realm of education, but in life, as a whole. Each of us is in a perpetual negotiation with the outer world. The way we navigate the dance between our personal styles and outer educational and social structures is a constant and ongoing challenge. My hope is that we can deal with this tension in a more humane, fluid, and life-affirming way.

Now, let's turn to the next chapter, where you'll have a chance to delve more fully into one of your own learning difficulties or "cracks" while working with people, and discover the special gifts of your facilitator style that are hidden within them.

CHAPTER 7

Your Cracked Pot Wisdom

"A broken line or an irregular curve is perfect in its very 'imperfection'" [25]

—D.T. Suzuki, Japanese author and translator

*I*N THE LAST *chapter, I spoke about learning difficulties as potential doorways to your unique style. In this chapter, you'll have a chance to explore and unfold one of those difficulties, or a seeming flaw or imperfection as a therapist* *or facilitator, and discover the gift it holds for your facilitator style.*

Have you ever said to yourself, "Gee, if only I could change this particular thing about myself, I would be a better facilitator! Why do I keep doing the same thing, even when I tell myself to be different? I thought I got past that problem a long time ago!" Or "Why aren't I as *perfect* as I'd like to be, in my work?"

Many facilitators complain to me that they learn many things, try to change themselves and do a better job or be like *others* who are better at their work. However, no matter what they do, they keep reverting back to their typical "imperfections"!

As we began to explore in the last chapter, in this chapter, you'll see how your seeming flaws, imperfections, or repetitive learning difficulties are keys to the unique qualities of your facilitator style. But before I tell you more, let me tell you a story.

The Cracked Pot Story

Have you heard the story of the Cracked Pot? Its origins are not completely known, but it is said that it came from India, or possibly from China. In the story, a water bearer carries two pots, each hung on the end of a long pole across her shoulders. One pot is perfect and the other has a crack. The perfect pot is very proud of itself for always delivering a full pot of water from the stream to the mistress's house. However, the cracked pot felt ashamed at its imperfection because it only delivered half a pot of water. It felt like a failure.

Seeing the cracked pot's distress, the water bearer asked it if it saw that flowers were growing on one side of the road. Apparently, the water bearer had noticed the crack and decided to plant seeds, which would always be watered, so flowers would grow as the cracked pot passed by. In this way, the water bearer could not only deliver water to her mistress, but flowers, as well.

The moral of the story is that the cracked pot's flaw, its leak, was actually *a gift* it had not yet recognized.

The cracked pot story teaches us that there are gifts hidden within cracks that otherwise seem problematic. Once again, Leonard Cohen reminded us, that it is just in the crack that the light can emerge. If we didn't have the crack, we might never see the light or jewels within it.

Cracks as Agony and Gift

There is no doubt that the cracks, or what seem like imperfections in our pots as facilitators, can be the source of agony, whether they emerge during the learning process or in the midst of working with others. Some cracks may have origins in persistent and painful social issues, parental scolding, difficulties with teachers, a sense of being "dumb" or incapable, etc. It can be very important to take time to work on these issues personally, and also collectively. At other times, it may be important to simply study things a bit more that you haven't yet grasped.

But as we saw in the last chapter, cracks such as learning difficulties that *persist over time* and that you can't *get rid of* contain the hidden seeds of some of the most important and unique qualities of your facilitator style. Yes, you can and will bypass them at times, but not permanently. If you could, you would be getting rid of some very special things about you that lie behind them; that is, aspects of your very basic and unique nature!

Think of it this way: you can try to be perfect or make yourself appear like everyone else. This could be important, at certain times. But, as Sarah Vowell, the author, social commentator, and humorist, said, "If I looked in the mirror someday and saw no dark circles under my eyes, I would probably look better. I just wouldn't look like me."[26] While "looking better" is not the point, the real goal is to bring out the gifts of your true and unadorned nature—just as you are. Deep within those "imperfections" lie special gifts that only you manifest, which will bring your work to life in your own inimitable way.

As I mentioned before, the idea that there is a jewel hidden within such difficulties is connected to a central Process Work idea that Arny discovered a long time ago. That is, within those things that are unusual, different, difficult, or unknown, are the seeds of wisdom. So, cracks in your facilitator pot are not there to be overcome or gotten rid of, but rather to be mined for their richness and creative potential. They contain the seeds of some of the most crucial and unique qualities of your facilitator style.

It might be comforting to know that there are many stories about well-known people whose teachers or parents gave up on them becoming anything in life, because they were somehow insufficient or "cracked." However, these individuals went on to become pioneers in their fields. Albert Einstein apparently did not speak during the first three years of his life. In fact, many of his elementary school teachers thought he was so lazy, he wouldn't ever become anything![27]

Canadian painter, Maud Lewis, had crippling rheumatoid arthritis as a young girl and went on to become one of Canada's best known folk artists.[28] Ludwig van Beethoven's teachers nearly gave up on him, because they felt he was hopeless and would never succeed with either the violin or music composition! The musician, Jay-Z, originally was not able to get any record label to sign him. Also, in his first screen test to act in a movie, the dancer and actor, Fred Astaire, was described by the testing director from the movie company MGM this way: "Can't act. Can't sing. Slightly bald. Can dance a little."[29]

Wounded Healer

Focusing on the "flaws" that seem to get in our way is particularly important for those in the helping professions. It may be that it is just *because of* the most unusual part of you, or difficult experiences in life, that you were driven toward your chosen profession—that is, wanting to make the world a better place for others. C.G. Jung described this phenomenon as the "wounded healer." He said the analyst is compelled to treat patients because she or he is wounded. This wound drives analysts to want to do something in the world, and at the same time, gives them the power to heal others. So, there is something dreadful about a wound, but it may also be the thing that gives you the resolve, passion, and feeling, to make a difference.

In a recent class, Arny spoke about the way in which our personal histories can bring great difficulties but also great powers, in the sense that *just because of those difficulties,* you know things that others don't. And it is often those difficulties that make you want to help and contribute to our world to make it better for everyone.

A musical version of the idea of the wounded healer can be found in the words of a great cellist, Gaspar Cassado. Cassado believed that going through difficult moments in life are essential for playing music well. At one point, he said to some of his students, "I'm so sorry for you; your lives have been so easy. You can't play great music unless your heart's been broken . . . very perfect technical control will not produce the most true sense and feeling of the music."[30] In other words, it is just because of the difficulties and imperfections in life that our true beauty and unique music can emerge.

Typical Facilitator Cracks

There are as many cracks or imperfections in facilitators' pots as there are people! However, there are typical cracks that I have seen in facilitators, therapists, teachers, and students around the world. These cracks sometimes persist over a long period of time, or appear suddenly and briefly. For some, the biggest crack has to do with a learning difficulty or inability to learn specific methods. Some facilitators speak about their crack as an inability to get out of their linear minds. Other cracks have to do with weird moods or trance-like states. Others speak of the inability to listen well or digest what the client is saying. Some facilitators are so intense and passionate, they feel that they overwhelm their clients. Many of my students have spoken about having a foggy or unclear mind when they are trying to be clear and linear. They describe this as going blank, feeling dreamy, fatigued, or unable to concentrate. (I'll speak even more about such noncognitive experiences in Chapter 20.)

Before going on to the exercise, take a moment to think

about one of your biggest "cracks" as a therapist/facilitator/ teacher etc, or student-in-training. For example, you might think of a troublesome state of mind/body, a cognitive or learning difficulty, a certain behavior, unusual feeling, or other crack that comes up in your work or learning process that . . .

- you can't quite overcome/change.

- comes up again and again, over time.

- disrupts your skills/learning or the way you would like to be.

- makes you feel unusual (not quite the norm).

- you might experience as a personal failure.

How do you experience that *crack*? What is it like? And how does it show up in your work or in your studies? Make a note, and then, let's go on to the exercise.

Notes about the Exercise

I'd like to give you the opportunity to explore one of your *cracks* in greater depth and discover the "light" or unique aspect of your facilitator style within it. First, let me mention a few things about the exercise.

I wrote this exercise as if you are actually working with a partner. However, you can do it alone, *imagining* that you are working with someone else. Again, please adapt this exercise to fit your situation, whether you are a therapist, group facilitator, coach, teacher, caregiver, etc. Set up the situation that will be most useful for you. If you are working with a partner, that person can lead you through the steps and play your "client" at certain points. However, please know that the focus will mostly be on *you* and your experiences. If you do work with a partner, that person's role is to guide you through the exercise and help you learn more about yourself and your unique style. In other words, *your* growth is the point! Your partner is in a dual role as both "client" and "helper."

You will choose one of your central and long-term "cracks" as a facilitator or facilitator-in-training and act it out. Then you'll begin to work with your partner (or imagine working with a client or a group). After a few minutes, I'd like you to sense if your crack or imperfection is somehow coming up spontaneously, inside of you. If it is, and even if it is not, you will then try to bring it consciously into your work, in some way. You'll take time to go deeper into that "cracked" experience by amplifying or intensifying it and discovering the gifts hidden within it.

For example, if your crack has to do with a recurring feeling of unknowingness when you work with others, go more deeply into that unknowing state. Try to relax and let yourself be *completely empty and unknowing.* If your crack has to do with feeling stuck in your linear mind, then become even *more* linear and exact. If you feel you are unable to notice the signals of the person you are working with, then *don't look* at anything they do and instead, notice what else you perceive. If you feel you are too energetic, *express this energy a bit more* to find out what it is trying to express. As you intensify your experience, I'll ask you to express it in terms of an imaginary or real figure, or piece of nature. After making a drawing of this figure/piece of nature, I'd like you to sense what gifts this figure might bring for your life and the style it is suggesting for your work.

Finally, your partner will, once again, act like your client (or you will do this, in your imagination) and you will imagine/try to use this new style with them and notice the effects. Be sure to make notes afterwards, about your experiences.

You'll need a piece of paper and pen for notes. Please know

that it is not important to do a "good" piece of work! Rather, the focus is on giving you the luxury to explore the light that wants to emerge through a crack in your facilitator pot!

Afterwards, I'll give you an example of the exercise from one of my class participants.

The Hidden Gifts within a Crack in your Facilitator Pot

1. What is your normal style of working? Act this out for a moment with gestures and words. Make a note about it. Now, identify one of your *cracks* as a facilitator that sometimes makes your work challenging. It may be a crack that comes up again and again. (For example, a crack might be a difficult mood or feeling, a troublesome state of mind/body, an "imperfection," a feeling of not being able to do or learn something, etc.) Describe what happens to you when this "crack" appears. What happens to your body, eyes, face, your focus, breathing, hearing? Act this out, for a moment.

2. Now, drop that experience and begin to work as you normally would with your client (or imagine working with someone). After five minutes or so, notice if your crack experience is around. If you notice it, and you are working with an actual person, then ask your client for permission to stop working with her or him and to focus on your own experience. If it is not around, please do this mechanically. That is, recall your cracked experience and take time now to focus on it (with the permission of your client).

3.   (Client, now help your partner go more fully into that crack with the following inner work.) Take time to feel, and then begin to express, that crack state experience. Feel it in your body, express it with movement, and add sounds and images, if they arise. Now *intensify* or *amplify* that experience a bit more, until you have a really good sense of it (be sure to take care of your body as you do this).

When you are ready, as you continue to move and express your experience, imagine that you are some kind of real or imaginary *figure* or *piece of nature* that is feeling and moving in this way. Who are you? What do you look like? Become this figure a bit more strongly and explore its mindset and feelings. Let it speak to you and tell you about itself. When you are ready, make a quick drawing of it and give it a name.

Act out that figure once again and sense the *facilitator style* this figure is suggesting for your work. In other words, ask the figure what style it would like you to bring into your work with people. Finally, imagine working with others using this style. What would that be like?

4.   When you are ready, turn once again to your partner (or imagine doing this with a client) and use this gift/style in some way as you continue to work with her or him. Let your cracked style inform and influence the *way you work* and *any possible skills* that you use, for about ten minutes.

5. Finally, discuss and make notes about the following:

    a. How did your cracked style influence your work? What gift(s) and special style emerged? How was it different from, or similar to, your ordinary style? What effect did it have on your client?

    b. How has this gift and style already been present in some way in your work? In other words, how has it been watering flowers in your work, although you may not have noticed or appreciated it? How has it appeared in other parts of your life?

The reason I ask if this experience has already appeared in other aspects of your life is that it is a central part of you that not only appears while you are working, but has been trying to get your attention throughout life. It is a central aspect of your deep dreaming process that wants to be recognized and appreciated. In other words, it has already been watering *a lot of flowers*, but you may not have recognized or valued its presence before.

An Example

Let me tell you an example of how I applied this exercise in one of my supervision sessions. My supervisee was a man who was a teacher in a small college. He described his "crack" in this way. He said he enjoyed instructing small classes, but was shy about teaching in front of larger groups. One day, he had to teach a larger group, and he became very tense and his mind felt almost numb. He had an uneasy feeling that his words were no longer making sense and he was afraid that he would start to speak but then would not be able to complete a full sentence! He somehow made it through the class, but wanted my help to find out more about this "noncognitive" moment. As he related the situation to me, I wondered what key to his unique style was hidden within this difficult experience.

I asked him to recall, and then re-experience that feeling of tension and numbness, and even amplify it a little bit; that is, to feel it a bit more. He tightened up his body and imagined that he became very numb. As he did this even more, I asked him what figure or piece of nature he might be. He said he felt as if he were becoming a very hard, solid, and grey rock. As he explored the rock further, he felt as if the rock had less and less connection with the outside world.

I asked him what the rock might say if it could speak. It said, "I'm just here. You have to take notice of me! I'm so big. I'm an old, stone boulder from high in the mountains that has rolled down to the valley. I am just here, with my perception!"

I then asked the rock what it would advise this man about his teaching style. It said, "You don't have to know everything!

Just use your perception. Take time, while speaking. Pause, when needed. There is no rush. Just stay centered and feel your body as this hard rock. It will know what to do. Build me into your teaching!"

This man was greatly relieved. Instead of feeling anxious and having to live up to some internal or external timing and standard as a teacher, he felt he could take his time, feel more solid within himself, and focus on his own perceptions. He imagined actually doing this with a class and then experimented with me, acting like his students. He went slowly and stayed connected to his inner timing, while following and teaching the course material.

When I asked him how this experience had appeared already in some part of his life, he said he had always loved to play in nature as a child. Later in life, he was drawn to meditate and hike alone in the mountains. There, he could follow his own rhythm and timing. This always brought a deep, inner sense of quiet and well-being.

In another supervision session, a therapist told me about a particular client situation in which she felt stuck. I tried to help her with cognitive information, but this approach did not work. She said that her problem was that she often feels blocked, like a "deer in headlights." In those moments, she feels unable to do anything at all! She said that this happens especially when her client criticizes her or gives her negative feedback.

I played out this situation with her, acting like the client who criticized her, in order to help her explore that blocked feeling. She felt paralyzed. I then asked her to simply report on what she was experiencing, while in that frozen state. She said, "I feel like I am collapsing, kind of dropping down." I encouraged her to follow that body feeling and drop down in some way, even more. Her body and head sank down. She then said that she felt like a witch who was meditating over her cauldron! I encouraged her to explore being that witch for a little bit and see what happens. As she did that, she suddenly began to have creative and colorful images of her client's situation that made sense to her. Earlier, however, she had not had access to it. Automatically, she then began to cognitively understand more about her client's situation. She realized that she had a gift of going deep inside and seeing magical and colorful images about her clients' situations!

When I asked this woman how this feeling and style had appeared earlier in her life, she said that she always loved to draw and sometimes made spontaneous drawings, which, afterwards would explain their meaning to her. You see, her "block" was the doorway into something she had always done: a gift of art and fantasy. She was now trying to integrate this gift into her work with others.

As you can see, it's very important to explore your persistent "cracks" instead of throwing them away or constantly trying to cover them up! In a way, these "imperfections" are saying, "I'm here and I'm not going away. I'm an essential, basic part of who you are. Please recognize me! I hold keys to some of your greatest powers and gifts for your work!"

Explore them so you can discover the light that is, and has always been, trying to come through.

Now, let's turn to the next chapter, where we will take all of this further and do something related, but a bit more radical! That is, you will *create* a new crack in your pot in order to discover special facilitator gifts that you may not have quite recognized before!

CHAPTER 8

You Might Gain If You Lose Something

. . . if one of our instruments breaks,
it doesn't matter.
We have fallen into the place
where everything is music.[31]

—Jelaluddin Rumi, Persian poet, theologian, and Sufi
mystic from his poem *"Where Everything is Music"*

I N THE LAST chapter, we focused on the wisdom behind a crack in your facilitator pot—those learning and practice difficulties that seem insurmountable, yet contain the seeds of your unique facilitator style. I want to remind you that if you can learn something through greater study and practice, please do! But if that stuck place, a learning block, or troublesome state comes back again and again, it is an important piece of your style. It is a gift that longs to be recognized and used.

If you ignore these cracks, they will persist and cause you to get exhausted, frustrated and incongruent, as you work. Yet, if you are more aware of the unique style that is trying to emerge, you will be more congruent in what you do, feel more at home, and have access to the unique nature that wants to express itself through you.

In this chapter, I'd like to take the metaphor of the crack in your facilitator pot one step further. I want to actually *create a new crack* in your pot and discover the hidden gifts for your work that lie within it. Let me begin by telling you the origin of these thoughts.

My Voice

When I was about to turn 40, I lost the upper range of my singing voice. I was very upset about that. Since I was young, I had always loved singing the tunes of my favorite artists, while accompanying myself on piano, dulcimer, or guitar. But as my fourth decade approached, I was suddenly no longer able to reach many of the high notes that had previously given me so much pleasure and passion. It was a huge loss for me.

In retrospect, I see that it was just that loss that opened a new doorway. That is, at the moment I was unable to sing the songs of others I admired, my *own* songs began to pour out of me. This was a great surprise, because until that time, I was completely blocked from composing my own music. From that moment on and until the present day, a musical muse has visited me innumerable times, inspiring me to compose a large body of instrumental and vocal music.

Three Strings

While I do not claim to be a virtuoso in any sense of the word, this experience reminded me of a story I read a few years ago, that was attributed to the brilliant violinist, Itzhak Perlman. At that time, I was pondering the direction of my next class on the unique style of the facilitator. I was struggling to find the path and my deepest intent behind giving this class. What did I really hope my students would gain, and learn about themselves? I knew I wanted to touch upon the fundamental core that moved and guided each person's work. I longed to explore the way our unique selves manifest, in terms of our personal facilitator style. I had a few ideas for the class, but I was a bit stuck as to how to go further.

As I pondered these questions, I became distracted by a bunch of mail that had arrived that day. The stack lay unattended on my desk for many hours. I aimlessly began to ramble through the envelopes, flyers, and leaflets. One of the papers in the stack was a newsletter which, without much thought, I began to toss toward the recycle bin. I had so many other "important" letters to attend to! However, just as I was about to toss it into the trash, my hand inexplicably drew the newsletter back towards me. I had a flickering intuition that it might contain just the inspiration I was searching for.[32]

Glancing hurriedly at the printed page, I was pulled toward a particular story. As I started to read it, my eyes suddenly filled with tears. I realized that it poignantly expressed the essence and spirit I was longing to convey in my class. After some investigation of the story, I discovered that it might not be completely true in everyday consensus reality! However, I discovered that the story had been repeated many times on the internet and elsewhere, and therefore, true or not, is like a fairy tale or dream trying to realize itself in the world. It has touched many people and expresses something profound which, I believe, many long for. So, with that in mind, let me tell the story now, and you can imagine it as a kind of fairytale.

In 1995, so the story goes, Itzhak Perlman gave a concert at Lincoln Center in New York City. On the night of that performance, the orchestra tuned up and was ready to begin. Perlman, who'd had debilitating polio as a child, walked on stage with braces on both legs and with the help of two crutches, took his seat. He released the clasps on his braces, tucked one foot in, put his crutches on the floor, and picked up his violin. When all of these tasks were completed, he then nodded to the conductor to begin.

Just as the orchestra began to play the first few bars of the music, one of Perlman's four violin strings broke, snapping so loudly that everyone in the audience could hear it. Ordinarily, a violinist in such a situation would get up and leave the room. She or he would get a new string or a replacement violin and then return to his or her seat in front of the symphony orchestra. However, in Perlman's case, this would have been too difficult and laborious.

Instead, Perlman sat quietly. He closed his eyes, and then signaled to the conductor to begin anew.

Now, if you know anything about a symphonic work, or can imagine it, it would be impossible to play the music with only three strings! However, Perlman insisted. So, the conductor began and the orchestra started again. Perlman played from where he had left off with incredible passion and beauty. Apparently, as the writer of the story related, Perlman modulated, changed, and re-composed the piece in his head as if he "de-tuned" the strings to create new sounds that had not been heard before.

When the symphony finished, everyone sat in suspended silence. And then, suddenly, great applause and stamping erupted. When the room was quiet again, Perlman said, *"Sometimes it is the artist's task to find out how much music he or she can still make with what he or she has left."*

I was so touched by that story, that it has stayed in my heart and mind for many years. It made me realize that while Perlman or any other skilled artist can have expert ability, and while each of us learns the tools of our trade, there is something else that takes over in the moment, when we "lose a string"— that is, a moment when something is unexpectedly taken away from us, such as the ability to use one of our central skills. In this case, the thing that took over when the violin string popped was the musician's artistry, which extended far beyond skills or musical notes on paper: the deep understanding and feeling for music that soars way beyond that which is known and practiced.

I meditated on this dream-story for a long time and on why it touched me so deeply. I pondered the moment when any of us loses something we rely on. What do we have left? When an artist, poet, teacher, therapist, coach, or facilitator forgets one or more of their tools, what do they have to fall back on? What takes over? Learned skills and methods can be extremely important for any particular discipline or art. Yet, who and what were there, before we learned those skills? Who is the original artist inside of each of us that emerges when we "lose a string"? What part of us comes forward and brings our "symphony" to life?

I realized, once again, that it is often in the unseen, deep powers on which we are *not focused* that we find the keys to our unique style. In that moment, I inadvertently discovered the focus of my class.

Over the years, I have told the story of the "Three Strings" many times in my classes. Though the story may not be true in the ordinary sense, I had always loved the beauty of Perlman's music, which I had heard over the years, and I have always felt moved to play a bit of his violin recordings during class time. Listening to his music, I find myself transported, connecting to the feeling and spirit of his style and artistry. I would recommend that you find some of Perlman's music and play it, as well.[33]

Losing a String

Like the violinist in this story, each of us learns a set of tools for our trade, whether we are musicians or therapists, counselors or organizational facilitators, coaches, religious or spiritual advisors, public speakers, artists, lawyers, teachers, business people, etc. Those skills might be highly technical or intricate. Musicians learn about melody, harmony, notes and chords. Therapists or coaches learn special skills of their particular school or approach to working with people. But when any of our practical skills are taken away, what is left?

In my classes, I began to explore what happens when any of us "loses a string;" I wanted to find out what gifts might emerge. What aspects of your special innate style might be revealed? For example, there may have been a moment in your own life when you "lost a string" in the sense of not being able to use one or more of your abilities or skills. While this can certainly be devastating, and I do not want to romanticize these events, there are sometimes fortunate moments when, because of this loss, something else was able to shine through. You may have sensed this quality within you previously, but had not grasped it fully.

Take a moment, now, to think of a time in your life when you may have lost something that was important to you. It is possible that you have not recuperated and do not see anything that came out of that terrible loss. That would make a lot of sense. However, just in case, look again and see if there *is* *something* that you gained; something that you didn't expect to manifest, that gave you a new direction, feeling, or task in life. Make a note and then, go on.

Stories of "Losing a String"

Before moving to the exercise where you'll have a chance to explore "losing a string," I'd like to share a few other stories about a loss and the unexpected gifts that subsequently followed.

Last night, I dreamed about Frida Kahlo, the great Mexican painter. After being severely injured in a bus accident at the age of 18, and while confined to a full body cast for three months, Kahlo occupied herself with painting. She had only dabbled in art, previously, as she had been aiming to go to medical school. Her mother gave her a special easel so she could paint in bed while she was recovering and her father gave her his own brushes and box of oil paints. A dominant theme of her paintings was the self-portrait. Kahlo said, "I paint myself because I am so often alone and because I am the subject I know best."[34]

Like Kahlo, there are many stories about musicians, martial artists, artists, dancers, etc., who have lost the ability to perform an aspect of their particular art, and as a result of that loss, discovered a gift. A striking example of this is found in the life and work of Ludwig van Beethoven. In this late 20s, Beethoven began to experience hearing problems and finally, in the last decade of his life, was almost totally deaf. He continued to compose, and astoundingly, some of his most beloved works, such as the *Ninth Symphony*, arose during the last 15 years of his life.[35]

There is a very touching story about the first performance of that symphony in Vienna. Beethoven was the conductor, but apparently, the players were instructed not to pay attention to him. They were told that Beethoven would be unable to conduct properly due to his great hearing loss. In a 1932 article, *Time Magazine* reported on this.[36]

Apparently, when the symphony concluded, a very poignant moment occurred. The audience began to applaud but, unable to hear the applause, Beethoven remained facing away from them, still looking towards the orchestra. He remained that way until one of the soloists turned him around so he could take in what was happening. "The demonstration took a sudden, emotional turn as the people started shouting, beating their palms together still harder in an effort to assure the fierce-looking little man of their sympathy, their appreciation."

When the anthropologist and spiritual teacher, Joan Halifax, was 4, a virus took away her sight and she was blind for two years. During that time, she discovered that she had an interior life. She says, of that time, "suddenly, another level of your life opens up when you recognize that actually, you have a life that is inside."[37]

The mixed media artist, Hanoch Piven, was rejected from art school. He realized that he wasn't very good at drawing or traditional "art." He felt that professionals did art, but he didn't, and he became quite depressed. After some time, he realized that a direct or traditional path to art didn't work for him. In fact, he thought that if he got off the *direct road*, he might find treasures. He realized that the search was not so much about technique, but finding his own way of doing things. Soon thereafter, he began to develop his own very unique and whimsical way of making caricatures, which are beloved around the world, today.[38]

The conductor, Benjamin Zander, could not continue playing the cello, which he loved, because he was unable to form calluses on his fingers. This set him off on a new track, whereby he discovered his great love and gift for conducting.[39] Similarly, as a teenager in Tokyo, Seiji Ozawa wanted to become a classical pianist. Defying his mother's commands, he decided to play in a rugby match, and proceeded to break two fingers—which ended his hopes of a piano-playing career. This, in turn, changed his life direction, opening a door that led to his becoming a world-renowned conductor.[40]

The Indian mystic, Inyhat Khan, speaks about the moment when he had to lay down his most beloved instrument, the Vina, and instead, let god play through him. "I gave up my music because I had received from it all I had to receive. To serve God, one must sacrifice the dearest thing, and I sacrificed my music, the dearest thing to me... Since then, I have become His flute, and when He chooses, He plays His music.[41]

Losing a "String" of Your Sensory-Grounded Channels

I hope none of you have to endure such agony and loss, and, as I said, do not want to romanticize these experiences. Nevertheless, these stories made me wonder: what would happen to us, as facilitators, if we were to *consciously* lose access to one or more of our tools or methods? What would be left? What might you gain, if you lost something? What aspect of your basic nature, style, and ability might appear through this crack?

In the next exercise, you'll have the opportunity to explore "losing one of your strings." You will drop one of the strings you tend to rely on as you work. Then, you'll notice the gifts that arise and what they teach you about your style. This experience has been very helpful to both students-in-training and long-time facilitators.

The "string" that you will "lose" is one of the sensory-grounded channels that you tend to rely on and habitually use in your work. The term *sensory-grounded channels* refers to the pathways through which we send and receive information. Some of the main channels that facilitators tend to use are the *visual* channel (seeing), the *auditory* channel (hearing, sound, and speaking), the *proprioceptive* channel (body feeling), the *kinesthetic* channel (movement), and the *relationship* channel (experiencing ourselves in terms of relationship interactions).

The reason I chose to focus on sensory-grounded channels is that the channels you tend to use while working are fundamental to your way of perceiving and understanding interactions. However, your use of particular channels may be so automatic that you ignore *other ways of perceiving.* The reflexive use of certain channels might also be due, in part, to *prescriptions* about *how to be* as therapists or facilitators. For example, many people in the Western Hemisphere and many others who live in industrialized countries (if they are not blind) tend to use their visual channel a great deal. Some facilitators are quite adapted, or especially related to, watching the feedback of the person or group with which they are working. This can be very helpful and important, but it can become so automatic that it blocks other channels of perceptions, talents, and abilities.

Therefore, by temporarily inhibiting your automatic use of specific channels, such as the visual channel, you may discover *other ways of knowing* that you have forgotten about or lost touch with.

Let me tell you a bit more about the exercise, before you try it. First you'll identify a sensory-grounded channel that you use habitually and then block it *temporarily*. For example, if you identify the visual channel as something you use frequently, you will block your vision in some way. You might, for example, *close your eyes* and not look at the person with whom you are working. If you tend to use your hearing or auditory channel quite a lot, then you might explore plugging your ears and *not listening* to what the other person is saying! This might seem a little strange, but the point is to find out what new types of perception arise. You can also explore *not moving or feeling* much, while working.

Then, you will imagine that you begin to work with a particular client or group (depending on your situation). If you do the exercise with a partner, your partner will be your "client." Once you block your habitual channel, simply notice what happens to you, as you work. What do you notice? And what, if any, new ways of perceiving and knowing emerge?

Personally, I have a tendency to use my eyes a great deal and sometimes, to overuse them! I have experimented with not looking at the other person and even putting a scarf over my head! I am a bit embarrassed to admit that some of my actual clients, who gave me the permission to try this with them, have said that these were the best sessions for them! They felt relieved that I wasn't looking at them with the typical therapist's empathetic stare which, at times, made them a bit uptight and unfree! In my experience, I noticed that I became much more attentive and sensitively tuned to the client's words and my own inner feelings than I had been before. I gained a lot of information I was not quite aware of, when I relied primarily upon my vision. I also realized that this way of perceiving is a gift that I have, but do not ordinarily utilize.

Another therapist who works with couples said he relies primarily on his auditory channel to listen intently to the content of what his clients say. When he experimented temporarily blocking his ears and not listening so closely, he became more aware of his own body movements. In fact, this man was very skilled in movement, but rarely used it when working with couples. He realized that he could be more animated while working. He imagined moving and acting out the clients' roles and experiences instead of relying solely on the clients to do all the work. He knew that he would then understand the content of what they were saying even more fully.

Of course, how you integrate this information is a creative task that is also based on the feedback of your clients. And ultimately, it is important to learn to *flow* with your ordinary channels and this new way of working and sensing. However, the exercise is primarily meant for you to have the time and freedom to explore the gifts that reveal themselves when you block one of your dominant sensory-grounded channels.

Please adapt the exercise to your specific situation and work, and give yourself the permission to be, or look, a bit silly. That is, if you want to, actually put a coat over your eyes or your fingers in your ears! I doubt you will do this with an actual client, but this experience is about exploring your own experiences. If you are working with a person in the role of your client, please thank your "client" for placing the focus mainly on you and your own learning as a facilitator.

Finally, if possible, try to stay *"half in and half out,"* as Arny and I call it. This means, stay close to your own experience, while still, in some way, noticing and adapting to the feedback and signals from your "client"!

Discovering Other Ways of Knowing: Losing a String

1. Act out the ordinary way that you work with people. Use your eyes, hands, and motions to express this manner of working. Study your behavior and identify the *sensory-grounded channels* that you tend to use the most (e.g., seeing, hearing, feeling, movement, relating). Make a note.

2. Now, block one or more of those main channels you tend to use. (For example, stop looking/seeing, stop listening, stop talking, stop moving, etc.). If you want, you might close your eyes, put a coat or a scarf over your head, put plugs or fingers in your ears, turn around and do not face the client, etc.

3. Now, begin to work with your "client" while in this "blocked-channel state" (or if you are doing this exercise alone, *imagine* doing this with a client) for a few minutes. Notice/imagine what happens to you. What sensations or perceptions, intuitions, tendencies, or experiences emerge? (If possible, try to be *half in and half out*, noticing and adjusting to your partner's feedback in some way.) After a while, if you want, you can begin once again to use your main channel(s).

4. After 10 minutes, discuss the following with your partner (or if you are alone, ponder to yourself).

    •   What was this experience like for you? What types of perceptions, feelings, experiences emerged? Did you use any sensory-grounded channels that you ordinarily don't use much?

> How was this different from your regular style
> of working?

- What special gifts, abilities, or parts of you
  revealed themselves?

- Did any spontaneous creativity emerge in you?

- Can you imagine flowing from your ordinary
  style with its typical channel(s) to this new way
  of working?

- Make notes about your learning.

- If you worked with a partner, that person
  should give you feedback about what you did.

Some Examples

Let me give you a few examples from my class participants.
An elementary school teacher said that she blocked her visual
channel. Ordinarily, she is quite disciplined with the children.
However, when she closed her eyes, she found that she could
listen more to what the children really needed and was able to
then join and support them more fully.

A therapist blocked his auditory channel and stopped
listening. As he did this, he realized that he began to listen to
himself more, to his own thoughts and feelings. At that moment,
he became very psychic and could guess exactly what the client
needed, even though the client had not said it directly.

An organizational facilitator said that he usually watches the
group and tries to catch each person's input and signals. He
said he also tends to get overwhelmed, feeling-wise, by all that
is happening in the group and wants to adapt to what everyone
is feeling. In the exercise, he blocked both his *sight* and also
tried to stop himself from *feeling* so much! He began to notice

his own impulses more and realized that he wanted to be more direct and incisive with the group. He tried doing this and it felt quite freeing. He was then able to return to his visual channel by noticing the feedback from the group and continuing with his skills.

Now, let's go on to the next chapter. There, I want to explore not only creating one crack in your pot, but doing something even *more radical!*

CHAPTER 9

Sculpture within the Stone

I saw the angel in the marble and carved until I set him free.[42]

—Michelangelo, Italian sculptor, painter, architect and poet

*I*N THIS CHAPTER, *I want to be a bit more radical and temporarily crack your pot completely! In that moment, we'll discover which special qualities of your facilitator style*

emerge. Once again, I'll tell you a story about why and where this idea originated from.

Forgetting Everything

More than 30 years ago, when we were living in Zurich, Switzerland, Arny and I, along with many friends and colleagues, began what would become a traditional five-week intensive course training in Process Oriented Psychology. In the very first course, I taught a class on Process Work theory.

As the final week of the course approached, I prepared a lot of material for the last class. I hoped to squeeze in as much information as I could, before the course was done! However, when I arrived at the class, I noticed that the fifty or sixty participants were quite tired from their very intense four weeks of study and practice. I realized that they might not have the energy, or room in their minds, for all the "important" theory I had prepared! In fact, I could imagine that any new information would simply squeeze into one of their ears and quickly fly out the other!

So, thinking quickly, I decided to abandon my earlier plans, entirely. Instead, on the spot, I developed what seemed, to me, to be a rather risky new and quite unusual exercise. I told them that I wanted them to experiment with *forgetting everything* they had learned over the past four weeks! In that moment, I noticed muffled giggles and visible sighs of relief.

To begin, I told half the class to drop all the knowledge they had accumulated! "Just let it go!" I said. Then, I asked them to turn to individuals from the other half of the group, who would act like their clients, and with their empty and blank minds, to now act as a therapist with her or his partner. "Just begin," I said, "and see what happens!"

I also shyly asked those who were acting like clients to grant the acting therapists permission to experiment, at least within limits! This was one of my more radical teaching methods, but it seemed appropriate for the moment, and considering the exhausted state of most of the students, was probably the *only thing I could do*!

As I watched them begin, many of the "therapists" sort of slumped down in their chairs with blank and unknowing looks on their faces. I started to get a bit worried. But then, I noticed they looked much more relaxed and freer than normal! Some of them began to play around like children. Others looked as though they were following whatever impulses went through them. And others sat silently for a long time, looking more at the ground than the other person!

These unusual "therapists" were more easy-going than they normally were, and I could tell they were freed from the inner and outer pressure to do something "right." At the same time, I was delighted to see that the "clients" seemed to be having more fun, too!

After about fifteen minutes, we gathered together and discussed what had happened. The results were quite interesting! Many of the therapists reported that when they dropped all their previous knowledge and skills, they actually became *more aware of* and *attuned to* what was happening with their clients. Most importantly, they were surprised that they felt as if their natural style of working (often hidden in the background as they struggled to learn and enact various methods) could now emerge in a more pronounced and easy way.

Some of the therapists said they felt deep inside themselves and, at the same time, closer than normal to the person with whom they were working. A man in the therapist role experienced his basic style as "clear perception," with nothing in the way. A woman was able to tune into things that the client did not say and pick up signals that she normally wouldn't notice. Interestingly, the clients also felt more relaxed and reported they felt that their therapists related to them more than normal! I was also surprised and delighted to hear from many who said that letting go in this way gave them an easier grasp of the skills they had been learning, and that they began to spontaneously use those skills in a more effortless way.

I began to wonder: what is really left, when you drop everything you've learned? What innate gifts emerge? What relational, artistic, and other special qualities are able to shine through, in those moments when you *crack your pot completely*? And how does this radical act influence the skills you have already acquired?

Your Default Function

I realized that our most natural and unique style can be understood as the thing we do without even thinking about it. It simply occurs in the course of me being me, and you being you. It is the "natural you," before and after various elements, tools, and skills are added or taken away. It is always there, regardless of the circumstances. It manifests in the background of all you do, whether used consciously or not. You probably recognize this part of yourself from childhood or other parts of your life, yet it may not be well known to you. As I mentioned previously, I sometimes call this part of us our "*default function.*"

I am reminded of the Zen concept of the *empty* or *beginner's mind;* the experience of perceiving the world, at least for a moment, without preconceptions. Indeed, the experience of forgetting everything is a goal in Zen and in other spiritual traditions. Of course, the students in our intensive course had acquired much theory and many skills they could always call upon, if needed, thank goodness! They are very important and helpful! However, as D.T. Suzuki said, "One has not understood until one has forgotten it."[43]

Impressive Therapists and Teachers

The experience in my class reminded me of some of the therapists, facilitators, and teachers who have impressed me most in life, either in person, or those I have heard about, through stories. I was astonished to realize that they rarely used their skills in the exact way they had learned them! Of course, some people I admire are excellent and skilled practitioners. And some of them blend their skills and personal style in  a seamless manner. At the same time, many of the teachers who really made an impact on me did not use the skills of their trade in the usual or obvious way; or even . . . at all!

I remember a story that Arny has told about one of his Jungian analysts, Franz Riklin, who had been the president of the Jung Institute in Zurich and was the nephew of C. G. Jung. I have always been amazed that, even though Riklin was a Jungian analyst, he never interpreted one of Arny's dreams (dreamwork being a cornerstone of Jungian psychology)! Rather, Riklin would focus on, follow, and talk about himself! Now, some people might think, "Oh, he's not relating! He is only thinking of himself!" But actually, by following himself, he was modeling connecting to Arny at a deeper level and believing in the dreaming and flow of the moment. In fact, this behavior was wonderful and very healing for Arny, as the client! I have noticed that when Arny tells such stories in his classes, many people begin to giggle and feel relieved, as if a world of possibilities suddenly appears![44]

Arny and I heard a wonderful story about forgetting everything, from a friend and teacher of ours, Keido Fukushima Roshi, who had been the Head Abbot of the Rinzai sect in Japan. Fukushima Roshi said that, one year, he came to the United States to lecture and give a calligraphy demonstration, but he forgot his brush. He had to go to a store to buy a new one. The next time he came to the U.S. for a demonstration, he forgot his paper. Again, he went back to the same store where he had bought the brush the year before.

This time, when he went into the store to buy paper, the storekeeper said, "Roshi, what will you forget next time?"

The Roshi replied, "Myself!" and laughed! What a wonderful story about the need to forget ourselves in order to remember our greatest art!

Forgetting Everything Exercise

The artist and sculptor, Michelangelo, is often quoted as saying that "inside of every block of stone or marble dwells a beautiful statue; one need only remove the excess material to reveal the work of art within."[45]

In the following short exercise, I'd like you to have the opportunity to "remove the excess material" from yourself, in order to discover the special art and artist within you. It is a slightly updated version of the exercise I gave 30 years ago.

You'll explore *what is left* when you momentarily take away *all that you have learned*, including your skills and theoretical ideas. That is, you'll explore the artistry, basic nature, and style that emerge, when you chip away the excess "stone." The steps are quite easy!

You can try this with or without a partner. It is also a fun exercise to do with a whole class. You can adapt the exercise to various situations, such as working as a therapist, teacher, coach, group facilitator, or any other type of helper. If you are working with a partner, ask that person for permission to experiment. If you are doing this exercise internally, imagine doing this with a client with whom you currently work.

1. Take a moment to relax. Relax your neck muscles, your head, your body, and allow yourself to simply drop all the ideas and concepts you have learned. Try to be totally empty, or as empty as possible!

2. When you are ready, turn to your partner (in reality, or a client in your imagination), and begin to work with her or him for a few minutes in this empty-mind state. Notice/imagine what happens. How do you feel? What do you do? How do you, or do you not, relate to the other person? Continue for five to ten minutes.

3. Now ponder/discuss these questions:

   • What did you do? How did you behave? How did this feel? Did you do, say, or notice things you may not have noticed before? Did you use any of your learned skills? What new experiences arose for you, and possibly for your client?

- Did you discover a central quality or feeling inside of you, that you somehow know, but are not often in touch with? What did you discover about yourself? What basic style emerged?

- If you worked with an actual person, get some feedback from your partner about her or his experience of your empty-mind way of working and being.

- Make notes about what you learned and the basic style that emerged.

An Example: Working with Organizations on Climate Change

I'd like to share an example that moved me deeply and unfolded in a surprising and special way. A man who was an organizational consultant, as well as an environmentalist, decided to do this exercise alone, imagining that he was working with an organization on climate change issues. He dropped all his thoughts and skills and became very empty. As he went deeper into that experience, he felt as though he was sinking under the earth. As he went further with this feeling, he had a strong sensation that the earth was *caring for him*. It was a very warm and comforting feeling.

He then had a sudden insight. He realized that he always feels that *he* needs to care for the earth. But this experience showed him that the *earth also cares for him*. As he began to think about the organization again, this experience gave him the feeling that he would begin working with them by dropping all his ideas and teaching methods. Instead, he would encourage people to first get in touch with *their own connection with the earth*. He felt that, only then, would it be easier and more effective to begin speaking about pressing climate issues and potential solutions.

Becoming Seamless

It's natural to work hard to learn the tools of your trade and even to strive for perfection. At the same time, there are moments when each of us can, or naturally do, drop all that we know, and follow our most unadorned, basic natures. Sometimes, in those moments, the techniques we have learned blend seamlessly with our personal style.

Sometimes this happens at the beginning of our studies, sometimes in the midst of studying, and often after many years of practice, when overt techniques soften and you begin to simply live in the flow of your nature and all you have learned. In those moments, you are no longer *doing* things, but rather, they happen seamlessly.[46]

It is similar to learning to ride a bicycle. At first, it can feel awkward and even scary, as you attempt to learn many adjustments and movements, while trying to keep your balance. Then, finally, you simply *ride*! And what a glorious and freeing experience that is!

Morihei Ueshiba, the founder of Aikido, "realized the true potential of his art only after he turned seventy, when he could no longer count on the power of his body."[47]

At that moment, the feeling and spiritual background behind his practice came fully through him. Kisshomaru Ueshiba, the son of Morihei Ueshiba, mentions a classical Japanese proverb that says, "Enter by form, and exit from form. Whether it be cultural arts or budo [Japanese martial arts], one should train and master form, but having mastered it, one should become free of it."[48]

On the other hand, a total beginner with a "beginner's mind" can sometimes grasp the beauty of a particular method, theory, or practice, in a fresher and more powerful way than more advanced students. In their book, *The Art of Possibility*, Rosamund and Benjamin Zander tell a story about the Russian composer, Igor Stravinsky, who once told a bassoon player that he was *too good* to play the very "perilous" opening to the *Rite of Spring*. The opening music expressed the "first crack in the cold grip of the Russian winter. . . ." Rather, Stravinsky said that this section of the music required someone with less training, who would strain every part of her or his abilities to do so. He noted that someone with greater technical ability would miss the expressive feelings of the opening of that piece.[49]

In any case, temporarily cracking your pot and discovering the gifts that emerge can bring a new spark to all you do and remind you of the hidden magic and natural wisdom of your unique style.

Being the Amazing Gaudi

A Short Vignette

" . . . originality consists in returning to the origin."

—Antoni Gaudi [50]

J UST NOW, MY *mind started to drift. I was feeling a bit tired and unfocused. When I let myself go into that feeling, I suddenly remembered something I had written some time ago, but didn't know where to put it in the book. I decided to follow that momentary "crack" and place it here.*

When I think of each facilitator's unique style and how it manifests in practice, my mind turns to Antoni Gaudi. Born in 1852, Gaudi was an architect and artist from Catalonia, in the northeastern region of Spain. He attended art school and then developed his own very unique style. Convinced that there are no sharp curves or straight lines in nature, Gaudi created buildings with bulges and curves, and spaces previously unseen in architecture.[51]

A number of years ago, Arny and I were in Barcelona. One day, we rented bicycles and found ourselves riding down a quaint street, lined with cafés. I remember gasping at a distant site that suddenly came into view. Rising high in the distance, we caught sight of the *Sagrada Familia*, arguably Gaudi's most famous creation. I was awe-struck to see this extraordinarily unusual structure, with its rippling curves and forms. It seemed to me as if it appeared out of some fantastical dream.

As we rode our bikes closer, our eyes lit upon a mass of tourists who surrounded the front of the building. They were all looking up with amazement at the church. Though unfinished to this day, *Sagrada Familia* is the most visited tourist site in Barcelona.

As we, too, goggled, with mouths wide open at the unusual architecture, I imagined Gaudi's process. He had learned many specific tools with which to create art and architecture. However, he obviously let his artist's sensibility and unique nature dream *into and through* those skills to produce this magnificent and unusual structure.

Sometime later, it occurred to me that each of our styles is somehow . . . well . . . *gaudy*! Each person's style is a unique combination of learned skills and their utterly unique, quirky, and outstanding nature. Aspects of your style might be as dreamy and radical as Gaudi's, or as linear and exact as a scientist. Most importantly, *who you are is the point: whether it is weird, unusual, special, overwhelming, magnificent, etc.* You will say that you can't be that way and that's why you keep it down. It might always feel as if it is too much in contrast to ordinary life. However, like Gaudi, your nature is irrepressible, and, I believe it is the source of the great artist inside of you.

As I stared up at the *Sagrada Familia*, I felt that Gaudi was teaching me another lesson; that it was possible, perhaps even crucial, to bring our special styles and artistry right into the middle of the hustle and bustle of everyday life. So, learn your skills while also nurturing the way nature moves through you and uses all that you know. Your special way of doing things is needed not only for yourself and your clients, but also for our larger world.

PART III
Your Artist's Palette: A Rainbow of Styles

*I*N THE FIRST *parts of the book, we have been exploring the facilitator's style in broad strokes. You had the opportunity to think about those things that make your style unique, as*

well as discover aspects of your style that are hidden; for example, within learning difficulties or "cracks" in your facilitator pot. Take a moment now to recall some of the experiences you had in the various exercises. Perhaps you will notice common threads that tie these experiences together.

Now, in this second half of the book, I'd like to put the concept of style in a larger theoretical context as we begin to differentiate it more fully. Finally, you'll have a chance to explore the larger flowing process and art behind your special way of working. In the moment, I notice that I am in a somewhat linear mood. Therefore, the chapters you will find in Part III will be a bit more didactic in tone!

CHAPTER 10

Substyles and Deep Democracy

WHEN I ASK facilitators to tell me about their styles, they usually speak in terms of the most typical or automatic way that they tend to work with people. However, if you look a bit more closely at the way you work with people, you would probably notice that you tend to flow between *a number of qualities or styles*. Sometimes, you might be very related and interactive with your clients or groups, while at other times, you might be more detached and directive. How can this be? Don't we have just *one* style?

Although it would be much simpler to talk about just one style of facilitation, in actuality, we all have a *diversity of styles*, or what I call *substyles*.[52] Some of these substyles are better known to us, whereas others are more hidden and further from our awareness. Most facilitators are not aware of, or tend to marginalize, certain substyles in favor of those ways of working that match their ordinary identities. However, each of us is multifaceted and has an array of substyles that contain the many rich qualities and energies that are basic to our natures. These substyles are like the variety of colors on an artist's palette that we all dip into and out of, as we work.

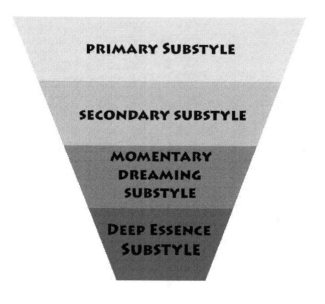

Without access to your full palette of styles and the flow between them, you will probably begin to feel that something essential is missing in your work. You will sense that you are cut off from your larger process and basic nature. You'll see, later in Part V, that these substyles are aspects of a larger process or facilitator's "dance" through which you flow, while working.

Your Substyles as a Rainbow

Another way to view your substyles is to think of a rainbow. Imagine that your overall facilitator style is like a prism. When you shine a light on it, a rainbow appears with a spectrum of colors, each of which indicates one of your substyles. Each color or substyle has its own qualities and feelings and is a fundamental force that moves or animates you, while working. For example, one of the colors of my own rainbow of styles has to do with being quite didactic, linear, and rational. Another color or substyle is very dreamy, artistic, and musical. Valuing each of these, and allowing myself to flow between them as they arise, have deeply enriched my ability to work with others.

Which substyle emerges in a given moment depends on many factors, such as the particular client or organizational situation, what's needed in a given moment, your own inner process, and so on. In any one session, one substyle may emerge, or many may arise.

My hope is to raise your awareness of, and fluidity with, the wealth and beauty of all your substyles; to learn to flow with them as they arise and to develop a loving attitude toward your overall facilitator nature. As the creative artist, Sandra Silberzweig, says, "I feel like a vessel allowing the message to be expressed through my paintbrush . . . I just surrender to its power and let go . . ."[53]

The Deep Democracy of Substyles

In the following chapters, I will introduce you to four different substyles that I call primary, secondary, momentary dreaming, and deep substyles. In order to understand them in a larger theoretical context, let me take a moment to briefly introduce you to Arny's concept of *Deep Democracy*.[54]

Deep Democracy points to an awareness of our multidimensional natures. That is, each of us experiences life through various *levels* or *dimensions* of experience. A deeply democratic attitude embraces all of the dimensions, seeing them as central to a full experience of life and, in this case, facilitation. Let me introduce those dimensions and how they relate to your substyles. I will say much more in the following chapters.

The first level is **Consensus Reality**. This level refers to the everyday reality that most people consent upon as real. It includes attention to everyday details, and the way you tend to identify yourself in everyday life and work. This level is connected to what I call your ***primary substyle*** as a facilitator.

In addition to Consensus Reality, there are other dimensions, which Arny called *dreaming dimensions.* These occur *at the same time* as you are focused on Consensus Reality and yet, are rarely noticed.

One of these dimensions is called **Dreamland.** This level refers to experiences that are dreamlike; that is, those experiences that lie in the background of your awareness and have been marginalized. Dreamlike experiences include, for example, feelings you have not yet noticed, dreams and dream figures, and double signals— meaning, body gestures that you do not identify with in a given moment. This level is connected to what I call your ***secondary substyle.***

Another dimension is the **Essence Level.** This level has to do with the most subtle or sentient experiences that can hardly be spoken about, and the feeling of being moved by the field or universe around you. This level correlates with the substyle that I call your ***deep substyle.***[55]

Here is a diagram showing these three levels and associated substyles.[56]

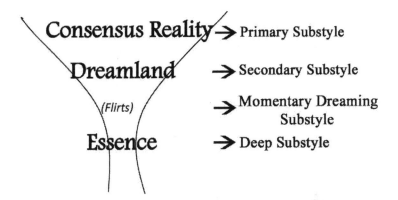

You will notice, between the Essence and Dreamland levels, that there is another realm that Arny called the **Flirt Level**. When subtle information from the Essence Level bubbles up into greater awareness, it appears first at the Flirt Level. This level has to do with the most fleeting experiences that quickly catch our attention, and it connects with your *momentary dreaming substyle*.

As the diagram indicates, the Consensus Reality, Dreamland, and Flirt Levels (and their associated substyles) seem to arise out of the Essence Level. The Essence Level (and its associated *deep substyle*) is like the *ground, or the mother from which all other levels and substyles arise*. In other words, the Essence Level contains them all, yet is larger and more encompassing than all the individual parts together.

In order to have a deeply democratic attitude toward yourself as a facilitator, you need to know about, and embrace, each dimension inside of you and the unique substyle associated with it. Without this willingness to know and hold all the dimensions, facilitators tend to become locked into one particular level or substyle all the time and do not have access to the rainbow of styles and gifts within them.

In the next chapters, you'll have the opportunity to learn about, and try, exercises to experience your substyles. You'll discover that some of the experiences you had in Part II are related to the deep substyle. I have reserved an entire section, Part IV, to explore this realm of your deep substyle in greater depth. Finally, Part V will help you bring all of your substyles together, discover their connection to your overall mythic path and pattern in life, and experience the dance between them, while working. With greater awareness of your inner style diversity, you'll be able to flow more fully with the natural powers and gifts that move you and ultimately feel more at home and congruent in your work.

CHAPTER 11

Primary Substyle

Client and Therapist[57]

*I*N THIS CHAPTER, *we'll begin to explore how your multidimensional nature expresses itself through your various substyles. We'll start by taking a look at your primary substyle,
the one with which you identify the most.*

Your primary substyle is characterized by the *main, automatic, or most predictable way* you tend to work with others.
It is the substyle that is closest to your awareness and mirrors

your *primary process:* that is, the ordinary or predictable way you tend to behave and identify yourself, over a given period of time.

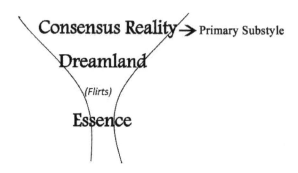

For example, if you identify with being very kind-hearted and attentive, your primary substyle as a facilitator will also be kind and attentive. Your primary process and its substyle arise out of the Consensus Reality Level and are often closely related to your upbringing and/or social norms.

Some facilitators have primary substyles that are empathetic, whereas others are linear and direct, formal, playful, etc. Arny has said that a typical primary substyle of many therapists can be seen in the way they hold their head and neck. Often, the head is tilted slightly to the side, in an empathetic and understanding gesture!

The Importance and Problematic Nature of Primary Substyles

Your primary substyle is a fundamental aspect of your nature and a powerful and important force in your work. In a way, it is the ground upon which much of what you do occurs. Cherish it and get to know it.

Get to know it? You might be wondering why I say *get to*

know it. "Isn't it related to the ordinary way I identify myself and therefore very known to me?" Actually, Arny discovered years ago that even though we identify with our primary process and substyle, it seems to *happen to us* unconsciously. That is, we tend to *automatically* or *predictably* behave in this way, without even thinking about it. You might, for example, habitually relate in a reserved or very friendly way, or perhaps in a formal way. It is so *automatic* that you aren't completely conscious of it! Even if it is something you cherish and value, you may feel that you have no control over it and are not able to free yourself from it, when needed. So, your primary style can sometimes feel like a compulsion!

In my book, *Alternative to Therapy,* I mention that many of us would like to change our primary substyles, because we are tired of being only that way! This is understandable and makes a lot of sense. However, a basic Process Work concept is that if something holds on and does not go away, it wants and needs to be used even *more* consciously. In fact, if you take some time to explore your primary substyle, you'll learn that it has great meaning and is reflecting a special aspect of your nature. (See the next section, below, for an example.)

Arny has said that we should never insult or criticize the primary substyle of a facilitator. It is a central and crucial part of her or him. So, appreciate this substyle and try to use it consciously. Once you do that, you will be able to let go and open up to other aspects of your rainbow of styles.

An Example of the Exercise

In the upcoming exercise, you will have the chance to explore your primary substyle and its deeper significance. Here is an illustration of the exercise, to first give you a hint about it. A female therapist said her primary and automatic style had to do with being open and warm-hearted with her clients. She said that this was also her ordinary, primary way of being in the world, which she liked, but also felt somewhat limited by. She complained that she would like to have access to other parts of herself while working with clients, but she just couldn't seem to change.

I recommended that she focus on, and then exaggerate, her primary substyle in order to find the deeper meaning behind it. She made a gesture to represent her primary and warm-hearted behavior. Her arms opened wide and at the same time she had a loving expression on her face. She intensified this feeling a bit more and meditated on its deeper meaning. She then realized that behind this behavior was an intense desire to make a warm home for everyone. She wanted her clients to feel good about themselves and to not have to endure a lot of self-hatred.

I encouraged her to stay close to that feeling and to sense the very essence or core behind this behavior and desire. She realized that it was extremely important to her that, in a world with so much pain, there was some oasis where people could relax and feel well. I then asked her to imagine a real or imaginary figure that could represent that feeling. She saw the image of Mother Theresa. As she took a moment to *become* Mother Theresa a little bit herself, she immediately had the feeling that each person is in the arms of something greater than her- or himself, something that cares for and supports them. She was very touched and said that this was actually a deep and guiding feeling that moved her in life and propelled her to become a therapist.

Then she realized, suddenly, that it was not *she* who needed to give this feeling to people, but rather, it was actually a feeling that people already had inside of themselves. This was very relieving to her and she felt she could bring this "knowing" more fully into her work with people.

She realized that without this deeper awareness of the meaning behind her primary substyle, she tended to stay a bit too much on the surface with people. That is, she was kind to her clients, but was not able to go more deeply and help people discover a supportive force or presence *within themselves*. With this awareness, she then felt freer to let go of it and use other substyles within her.

Exploring Your Primary Substyle

In the following exercise, you will have the chance to appreciate, embrace, and even amplify or exaggerate the qualities of your own primary substyle until you know the deeper significance behind it. You'll express this feeling with a movement and an image of a real or imaginary figure and then draw a sketch of that image. Finally, you'll ponder the gifts that this style brings to your work.

This exercise is a form of innerwork in which you will imagine that you are working with a client, coachee, group, teaching something, or whatever configuration is useful for your particular work and situation. It is also fun to do the exercise with a partner who will act like your client, or even with a small group that could act like a group or organization with which you work.

Discovering and Amplifying Your Primary Substyle

1. Depending on your situation, imagine working for a few minutes with a client, teaching something to students, facilitating a group interaction, giving a coaching session, etc.

2. After a few minutes, stop and consider what your primary substyle of working has been, until this point.

    a. How would you describe your primary substyle? What qualities does this style have? How does it feel? How do you move? How do you use your hands, your eyes, your body posture?

    b. Express this primary substyle quality with a simple hand or body gesture/motion.

3. Now *exaggerate that primary substyle* a bit (e.g., if you are primarily attentive, then be even more attentive!). You may be shy about it, but try as best as you can to exaggerate your motions, the sound of your voice, the feeling that you exude, etc.

    a. After a minute or two, take some time to sense the *core* or *essence* of this way of being. That is, what is it *really* trying to express? Where is it trying to go? What is its deeper significance, or the hope that is behind it? Make a note.

    b. Now, imagine a real or imaginary figure who would have this behavior. Who would it be? When you have a sense of a figure, become it, yourself. Feel like that figure; take her, his or its posture; hear or speak the figure's voice, etc. As you do that, sense any new information this figure might bring, about the significance of this primary substyle.

    c. Finally, imagine how you could use this substyle even more consciously and usefully in your work.

Using Your Primary Style and the Field Between You and Your Client

Let me close this chapter by bringing a different angle on the importance of being conscious of your primary substyle. Think of a therapist who said that his primary substyle was to be attentive and good-hearted. He said that he would like to be more direct, but was not able to do that. He also said that he tended to inhibit and not speak about some of the uncomfortable feelings he sometimes has when he is with his clients.

His supervisor told him that he needed to bring his discomfort into his therapy sessions more often. However, no matter how hard he tried, this therapist always ended up acting in a sweet and kind way towards his clients.

What could he do? Instead of changing this behavior, the man could make his primary substyle conscious by bringing it out more fully in his work. He might say to a client, for example, "Did you notice how parental I am being? I just noticed it and I hope it's having a good effect." Or, "I notice that I want to intervene more strongly, but I am feeling so parental that I am unable to take a stand. Do you perhaps need protection? Do you need a parent?" It is possible that this is exactly what the client needs, or perhaps the client will react and say that she or he actually needs something very different.

So, if you want to put your primary substyle to the side but are unable to, it may be that it is an important role in the field between you and your client that is seeking more awareness. If you make it conscious and explicit, it might help to clarify the field between you.

It is important to notice your primary substyle and to

use it consciously. It can help you sense and use the deeper significance behind it, potentially clarify the field between you and your clients, and ultimately give you greater freedom to flow with other aspects of your facilitator style.

CHAPTER 12

Secondary Substyle

A Facilitator's Primary and Secondary Substyles[58]

*I*T'S NATURAL TO *identify with certain parts of ourselves and not with others! As we saw in the last chapter, each of us has a primary process we identify with, which forms the basis of our primary substyle. At the same time, there are other parts or energies inside of us that seek our attention and want to be used in our work. With a more deeply democratic attitude, you can begin to embrace these experiences and the rich qualities they bring to your rainbow of facilitator substyles.*

Your Secondary Substyle

Whereas your primary substyle is close to your awareness and identity, your *secondary substyle as a facilitator, teacher, therapist and so forth,* is further away from your awareness and, therefore, less known to you. It is connected with your *secondary process,* which refers to the signals and experiences with which you do *not* identify. These experiences seem to *happen to you.* For example, if you primarily identify as a very shy person (like the facilitator on the left side of the cartoon, above), you might not identify with, or you tend to ignore, expressive signals and energies that happen spontaneously inside of you (see the figure on the right side of the picture). As you'll remember, your secondary substyle is related to the Dreamland Level of Deep Democracy. (See the diagram.)

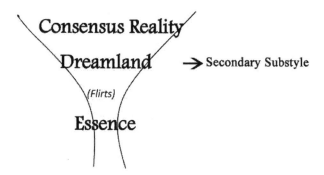

You may wonder if you have just one secondary process and style. Your secondary process and its associated style do change, depending on where you are at in your life, your inner development, etc. However, if you study yourself over time, there is often a secondary energy that comes back again and again, that you tend to marginalize. You will see, in Part V, that this returning energy is mythic for you: meaning, it's part of a long-term pattern, over your entire lifetime.

The Facilitator's Secondary Process

Facilitators experience secondary processes in the form of spontaneous experiences that arise while working. These can include such things as disturbing body symptoms, double signals, and inner voices. If you look more deeply into, and unfold, these experiences, you will discover that the qualities and energies they contain are the seeds of your secondary substyle.

Here's an example. A therapist I once supervised had a primary substyle of listening intently to the content of her clients' lives. She did not want to interrupt what her clients were saying, but rather, felt it was important for them to speak as long as they wanted and needed to. This style was wonderful and appreciated by many of her clients. However, she sometimes felt that she was not quite getting deep enough in her work.

She complained that, while working, she frequently experienced a body symptom that disturbed her; some of her muscles tended to become tight and clench up. I asked her to show me what that tight clenching sensation was like. She expressed it with a tight fist. When she meditated on the fist, it felt as though it were expressing a very tight and focused awareness. I then asked her what (secondary) substyle this experience might be suggesting for her work. She said it suggested that she be a bit firmer, in the sense of intervening more quickly with her clients. That would mean not listening quite as long as she ordinarily does with her clients, but rather, jumping in earlier, in order to make suggestions. If she were able to do this, she would pick up the energy that her symptom was suggesting for her work and would also feel more congruent.

In one situation, this was crucial for her work with a particular client. She spoke about one of her clients who had trouble getting things done in his life and being direct in relationships.

The therapist realized that this client may not be helped sufficiently if she, the therapist, were connected only to her receptive primary substyle. Rather, the client might *benefit* from the therapist's being a bit more directive and interventive. Why? This would model a needed energy for that client, as well.

The Edge between Substyles

All of us therapists and helpers, like all people, have secondary processes that are different from our primary process identities and substyles. That does not mean we *try* to be *split* or *incongruent*! Rather, it is a *natural* part of all human beings, to have other parts of ourselves happening simultaneously! We are always growing. We naturally identify with one aspect or dimension of ourselves, while other, more marginal parts of ourselves that are new or unknown are continually emerging and broadening our identity.

The boundary between your primary and secondary substyles is what Arny calls the *edge*. When you are at an edge, it can feel like standing on a precipice, afraid to step off into new territory!

How you move with, and manage, the *edge* is a creative task and depends entirely upon your process, the moment in time, and your client's situation. A process oriented approach would value and try to flow with your primary and secondary styles and the edge, as each arises.

Sometimes, therapists are at an edge to bring in their secondary substyles, because they fear they will lose their awareness. In some respects, this might be true! You may not have much practice flowing with the more marginal, deeper experiences that move you. However, if you *don't* follow the deeper experiences that are trying to come to awareness and enrich your work, they might *block* your ability to use your normal skills (as we explored in Part II)!

Learning to flow with all of your substyles and states of mind is a matter of personal training and development. Learn your skills and practice flowing with other dimensions of your experience.

Discovering Your Secondary Substyle

Let's begin to explore your secondary substyle. I will offer a couple of exercises to get in touch with this substyle. You'll have the chance to explore your double signals and also inner critics. Let me first mention two other simple ways to discover an aspect of your secondary substyle.

First, simply ask yourself what type of energy you tend to marginalize again and again, in your life and work. You somehow know this energy—in fact, you do use it occasionally, but you are shy about it. The therapist above, for example, said she knows that, over time, she tends to marginalize her more incisive and quick energy.

Another easy way to discover your secondary substyle is to ask yourself a simple question. That is: "If you were totally free, what style would you have, right now?" This can quickly bring up a secondary style that you have marginalized. Arny and I have playfully called this your *Anti-Style*.[59]

Finding Your Secondary Substyle in Double Signals

Let's discover your secondary substyle through a *double signal* that arises while you are working. To reiterate: double signals refer to body signals, gestures, and experiences that do not go along with your momentary intention, or primary process and substyle. You can notice double signals in many ways, such as the way you use your posture, the use of your eyes, your voice tone, etc. You can also notice things like the direction your body is facing. For example, you might identify with being very attentive, but notice that your body is turned slightly away from the person or people with whom you are working.

To discover your secondary substyle, you can simply amplify a double signal until you sense what it is expressing and what secondary substyle it would suggest for your work.

Before you try the exercise, let me give you an example. In a supervision session, an organizational consultant told me that he was having problems with his energy while working with organizations. He said he primarily wanted to use his mind to understand and facilitate what was happening, but was frequently exhausted during and after the sessions. He tried not to appear tired while working, but it was hard to do! His body often felt very heavy, and he noticed that his shoulders seemed to cave in a bit, while working. This sense of exhaustion is a secondary, double signal. Even while telling me about this dilemma, his voice tone was very low and lackluster.

I suggested that he imagine what would happen if he followed his sense of exhaustion. He welcomed the idea right away, saying he would sit back and relax in his chair. I encouraged him to do that, now, in the moment. He immediately leaned back, took a big breath, shut his eyes, and said that he felt really well. I encouraged him to follow that feeling, to enjoy it, and see what happened.

After a few minutes, several thoughts and ideas about a particular organization he was having trouble with emerged effortlessly in his mind. He spontaneously began to have a clearer idea about the process between himself and the group and new ideas began to pop up about how to work with them. He was delighted by this new secondary substyle and said that it felt quite natural to him, though he had never allowed himself to experience it fully.

His *edge,* or hesitation to follow that sense of tiredness while working, had to do with his primary substyle of being very logical and clear. He now realized that his exhausted feeling was the carrier of a different form of intelligence. If used consciously, this secondary substyle could bring up new ideas he was not able to find with his ordinary consciousness.

About the Exercise

In the following exercise, you'll have a chance to explore one of your double signals, as a key to your secondary substyle. Once again, you can do this exercise alone, imagining that you are working with others, or do it with a learning partner. For ease, I will write the instructions as if you (a therapist) are working with a partner (who is playing a client).

As in previous exercises, if you do the exercise with an actual partner, your "client" will have the dual role of also helping you follow *your own process* more deeply. The focus, therefore, is more on you, than on helping the "client." Again, please adapt all of the exercises to your particular situation; that is, set it up so you are working as therapist and client, facilitator and group, coach and coachee, teacher and student, etc.

For training and learning purposes, I'd like to give you the freedom to experiment fully, expressing the style that your double signal is suggesting. Ultimately, how you bring in your secondary substyle depends entirely upon the moment, your inner process, and the client's feedback. As I have mentioned earlier, Arny and I have found that it is most helpful, finally, to remain *"half in and half out,"* which means *half inside* of yourself, exploring the style and experiences that are emerging, while at the same time *half outside*, watching and adjusting to the feedback from those with whom you are working.

Discovering Your Secondary Substyle in Double Signals Exercise

1. You are the therapist and your partner is the client. (Or do this alone, imagining that you are working with a client.) Therapist, start to work with the client. After a few minutes, notice and describe your main, primary substyle of working (for example, being kind, exact, attentive, motherly, directive). Notice what body signals, gestures, posture, etc. go along with this primary behavior. Exaggerate this primary way of working and speak about why this way of working is so important for you.

2. Now continue to work with your client (or imagine working with a client) and after a few minutes, notice one of your *double signals* that does not go

along with your primary intention and style (for example, an unusual tone in your voice, a body posture or signal that does not go along with your intention). Speak out loud about what you notice.

3. Now, your partner-client will lead you through the following innerwork. Amplify your double signal a little more. That is, exaggerate, or make that double signal a bit more intense. (For example, if your body is slightly turned away, then turn away even more.) As you do that, meditate on what this experience is trying to express. Then, ask yourself what secondary substyle this experience is trying to recommend. (For example, if you turn away more completely, perhaps this is advising you to be more deeply inside yourself and not focused so intently with your eyes on the other person.) Make a note about your secondary substyle.

4. When you are ready, use this new substyle for a few minutes in some *creative and natural way,* as you work further with your client. If possible, stay *half in and half out,* following yourself, while noticing the client's feedback and adjusting accordingly.

5. Finally discuss:

    •   What did your momentary secondary substyle add to your work? How did it feel? Did it change/enhance your primary way of working? Did it bring any new creativity to your work? What are your edges to this substyle? Can you imagine noticing and identifying with this substyle a little more in your work and possibly in your life?

- Did your experience give you more access to your learned skills and/or did it create any new skills? Did it connect in some way with your client's process?

- "Helper-client," please give feedback to the therapist.

Let me give you one more example of the way in which double signals inform a facilitator's secondary substyle. Arny was supervising a group process facilitator. The man said he was quite open and was trying to use his skills diligently. This was his primary substyle. However, he said he was frustrated, because he felt he could not "hold things down" enough, when important or emotional moments occurred in groups. As he spoke, he made a strong definitive cutting motion with one of his hands.

At that moment, Arny said to him, "Yes you can. You can hold things down! I just saw you do it with your hand!"

The man laughed, realizing that he had just made that double signal with his hands and was shy about it. He made the motion again and then visualized bringing that definitive energy into an emotional group situation. He imagined that he would, at a certain point, say to the group, "I feel the topic that has just come up is really important. I don't know why, but I feel we need to stop here for a moment!" This was a big relief for him and he also sensed that the organization would be relieved to focus more deeply and intently on their issues.

Finding Secondary Styles in Inner Critics!

OK, I hate to say this, but one of the ways that secondary energies, particularly intense and forceful powers, arise while you are working is not only in body signals and disturbing symptoms, but sometimes in the voices of *inner figures or critics*! I have definitely experienced this! As a result, I placed an inner critic puppet that I bought near my chair in my office. I have even spoken to this rather undesirable figure in moments when it has bothered me while working, rather than simply being plagued inside of my head! I sometimes introduce this critic to my clients, and other times, keep the whole thing to myself and do the innerwork internally.

Of course, many students-in-training and even long-time facilitators have inner critical voices and figures. I have noticed these figures emerge often during "live" supervision sessions in which a therapist or facilitator is demonstrating her or his work with a client/group. I can sometimes tell by the way the facilitator is working or asking me questions that an incessant critic is giving her or him a hard time. It is making it difficult for the facilitator to continue working, or to even have a meaningful discussion about what is happening!

You may be aware of such an unrelenting judge that constantly evaluates your work. It is a terrible and bothersome burden. Yet, at the same time, paradoxically, these distasteful voices can often hold the seeds of your momentary secondary substyle! How? For example, a student was practicing her therapy skills with another student during a supervision session. I noticed that this student-therapist looked uneasy from time to time. She said that an inner critic was telling her that she was doing a bad job. I recommended that the woman *become* that critic and speak its thoughts.

*Inner Critic
(clipart image)*

The critic was quite nit-picky and pointed out everything he thought the student was doing wrong . . . and there were a lot of things! This critic was quite familiar to this woman, and she said that "he" never says anything about what she is doing right!

I encouraged her to act like the critic a bit more, and then, to drop its form and to simply feel and make its motions and energy. She stood very tall, pursed her lips, frowned and looked down as if she were superior to everyone. She said she felt she had an enormous, powerful energy. Then, she suddenly realized that she could use that energy, herself! She was often shy, tentative, and unsure of what she was doing. As she used her awareness to explore this energy further, it began to transform and finally crystallize into the quality of "knowingness." That is, *she knew the way!* She was a bit embarrassed, but tried to use this secondary substyle with her client. She began by sitting very tall and looking "smart," and as she continued, she relaxed and realized that she has a lot of inner wisdom but never quite believes enough in it. This was very relieving. Afterwards, I encouraged her to practice flowing between her primary and her secondary substyles, as they arose.

I have to add that sometimes you simply need to fight off your critic and tell it to back off! Paradoxically, by taking a stand, you actually pick up the critic's power in a useful way! Then, you can see how you would like to use that newly found energy, as part of your secondary substyle, in your work.

OK, here's an exercise to explore an inner critic and the secondary substyle that might emerge from it.

Inner Critics and Secondary Styles Exercise

1. Recall an inner critic that plagues you from time to time while you are working, or imagine such a critic, now.

2. What is that critic like? Feel your way into her/him/it. Take its posture, make its gestures, and speak its (critical) words.

3. Amplify this behavior—that is, express it a bit more strongly in order to get a good sense of this type of energy.

4. Now, still feeling the intensity of that figure, make just the motions once again, without speaking and sense the *essence* or impulse behind that energy. What is it trying to express? How might you need this type of energy in your daily life? Finally, imagine the secondary substyle this experience would suggest for your work and imagine using that secondary substyle in a useful way, with your clients.

5. Make notes about your learning.

As you begin to notice and use your secondary substyle, you will have access to more of the rich qualities and gifts of your artist's palette and you will feel more congruent in your work.

Now let's turn to your momentary dreaming substyle.

CHAPTER 13

Momentary Dreaming Substyle

*I*N THIS CHAPTER, *I'll introduce you to what I call your momentary dreaming substyle and offer some exercises for you to experience it.*

In contrast to your somewhat predictable primary and secondary substyles, your momentary dreaming substyle emerges in brief moments when fleeting experiences cross your path, as a facilitator. These experiences can temporarily influence your style of working and bring new information to your work. Many of you are probably very gifted in following your momentary dreaming experiences, but may not have identified them as such.

Momentary Substyle, Flirts, and Deep Democracy

In the diagram of the levels of Deep Democracy, you will notice that the momentary dreaming substyle is located at the level of "flirts," just above the Essence Level.

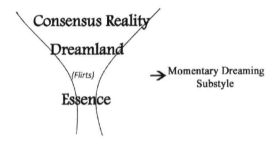

Now, if I were you, dear reader, I might protest, saying, "Wait a minute! We can't 'flirt' while facilitating!" And, of course — that's right! However, here, the concept of *flirts* is quite different than the ordinary interpersonal way we think about it! Arny uses this word to refer to fleeting nonverbal sensations, visions, sounds, moods, hunches, etc., that occur so rapidly that you almost don't notice them with your awareness.[60] For example, your attention might be caught for a split second by the brilliant color of a flower outside your window and then immediately forgotten, as you return to the work at hand. Flirts can happen in any sensory-grounded channel. There are visual flirts, auditory flirts (such as quick sounds that catch your attention), movement flirts (brief and subtle movement tendencies in your body), as well as others. Flirt-like experiences are of such brief duration that we normally do not hold on to them long enough to unfold them into consciousness, or to even express them in words.

So, how do you notice a "flirt-like" experience while working with others? To do this, you can become aware of those moments when something briefly catches your attention, then focus on it long enough to discover what it is trying to express, and the style it is suggesting for your work, in that moment. You can also *consciously* decide to seek and notice a flirt. To do this, you need to drop into a special type of attention, which Arny calls "lucidity."[61] This means assuming a slightly dreamy or foggy state of mind and while in that state, notice tiny, fleeting, "pre-signal" experiences that catch your attention.[62] Using your lucid attention can be especially helpful when you feel confused and in need of more information about the situation with which you are working. I will give some examples, shortly.

Scribbling and Your Dreaming Substyle Experiment

Before I say more, I would like you to try something I sometimes do with students, therapists, or other types of facilitators, just before I begin to supervise their work. I like to do this in order to ask the dreaming world what it would like to say about the upcoming supervision and the facilitator's style. I assume that, in addition to our conscious minds, the dreaming world also has important information that will enrich our work together.

I would recommend that you sometimes try this experiment

just before you work with someone, or do supervision, in order to discover something about your momentary facilitator dreaming substyle. It's fun and just takes a couple of minutes. You'll need two pieces of paper and a pen.

OK, recall and meditate for a moment on your primary substyle of working as a facilitator. What are you normally like, when you are working with others? Make a note about this.

Now, take a moment to relax; relax your body, let go. Let your mind and your eyes become a bit blurry and foggy. And when you are ready, still in this foggy state, take a pen and make a quick spontaneous scribble on your paper. That is, without thinking, let your hand quickly make a nonsensical squiggle. (For example, see my scribble in the picture to the right.)

My Scribble

Now, still in your foggy-mind state, gaze at your scribble with blurry eyes and notice something about it that quickly catches your attention. You might notice a special line, a shape, or perhaps an image that appears in part of it. When you are ready, draw just this line or shape that caught your attention, on another piece of paper. Then use your pen to bring out more fully whatever it is that you saw.

When you are done, ask yourself what this thing you saw/drew from your scribble might be suggesting for your facilitation style. That is, what might this figure, feeling, or energy, add to your style of working with others? What substyle is it suggesting? Make a note about this and notice how this new suggestion about your style is similar to, or different from, your ordinary or primary way of working.

Let me tell you about my experience. My primary substyle is often quite related, warm-hearted, and open to the people with whom I work. My eyes tend to be open and I try to follow what the other people, or person, is saying. When I gazed at my scribble, I saw in one of the curved lines, the beginnings of an image of a woman who was quite inward. I filled in the drawing of this woman on my paper (see

Inward Woman

my drawing to the right). When I meditated on this figure, I realized that she would be quite inward and pick up on slight visions or intuitions inside of herself. This was a new style that I am normally not identified with, that wants to be incorporated more fully and consciously into my work.

Ways to Notice Flirts and Access Your Momentary Dreaming Style

There are a number of ways you can notice and explore flirts and the momentary dreaming substyle it is suggesting for your work. I will name a few, here.

Catching a Flirt Before You Start Working:

This method involves noticing a momentary dreaming substyle that is trying to emerge, even *before* you begin your work! That is, catching a flirt before you start working with a client or group. Here is an example. Before I began to work on the phone with a client one day, my eyes lit upon a picture on my wall of a mountain where Arny and I like to go skiing. I meditated on the mountain and imagined it saying to me, "When you don't know what to do, ask Mother Earth. She will tell you what to do." I brought this into my work with the client by taking more time to wait for Mother Earth to guide and show me what to do.

Here is another example. I was supervising a man who was an organizational facilitator. As he entered my office, and before he even began speaking about the organizational situation he was seeking help for, he quickly glanced at a guitar that was propped up in the corner. He made a brief comment about liking that instrument and then began to tell me about the organization. I encouraged him to, first, keep his attention a bit more on that flirt and dream more deeply into it. He said the guitar brought him a deep musical feeling. He then realized that the problem he was having did not have to do with needing more knowledge about the group. Rather, he realized that he needed a more *musical style* while interacting with them. How would he do that? He said he would flow more with the organization's process and facilitate with a more musical and lyrical feeling, rather than his typical linear approach.

Noticing Flirts Spontaneously Arising While Working:

Another way to discover your momentary dreaming style is to notice a flirt that spontaneously arises *while you are working* with people. Many of us are so focused on the interaction with our client(s) that we ignore fleeting experiences that cross our attention. Yet, these quick flirt-like experiences can bring much needed information about the situation, as well as recommendations for your momentary substyle.

I was working with a woman who was a counselor who worked mainly with individuals. She felt a bit stuck in her work, but didn't know why. She spent a lot of time describing some of the inner problems that arose inside of her, as she worked with various clients. At one point, I was briefly distracted by a lovely tree I saw outside of my office window. Without telling her, I quickly used my lucid attention to imagine more deeply into that tree. I especially noticed how the roots sprawled outwards. I allowed that image to influence my momentary style and told the woman that perhaps she needed to widen her viewpoint about her work. To my surprise, this really resonated with her. She said that, while her work was interesting, she felt she needed to expand what she was doing, to focus more on collective social issues and groups in her community.

I am reminded of a story about C. G. Jung that stresses the importance of following flirts and momentary dreaming experiences. In this story, the flirt was a fleeting auditory experience. Jung had a client with seemingly incurable insomnia. While with this client, Jung suddenly remembered a lullaby that his mother sang to him as a child. The song was about a girl in a boat, on a river that had sparkling fish underneath. He let this song influence his style in the moment, as he began to hum the song out loud. The song apparently brought the sense and feeling of the rhythms of water and wind, and enchanted his client. From that point on, her insomnia vanished! Jung had listened to a fleeting experience inside of himself and by allowing this to manifest, connected deeply to his client's process.[63]

Consciously Seek a Flirt:

Finally, you can *consciously seek a flirt* when you feel confused or bored, or need more information while working. First, assume a lucid, foggy state of consciousness, and then simply look around and notice what catches your attention. For example, I was working with a teacher who was really frustrated and stuck with one of her lesson plans. I felt a bit stuck as well, as her therapist, and decided to look around and see what caught my attention. My eyes lit on a picture of a baby that I have in my office. I then said to the woman that perhaps she needed to be a big baby and throw a fit first, before she could complete her plans. She really liked this and said that, actually, she did feel a little bit like a four-year-old kid who was in a bad mood. She proceeded to make funny faces and act like a grumpy child and I joined her. After that, she felt much freer and was able to plan her class in a more fun and spontaneous way.

You can also seek a flirt happening in your body, in the form of slight movement tendencies. We'll explore movement tendencies later in the chapter.

As always, the way you notice a flirt and how you incorporate its message(s) into your work depends entirely upon the momentary situation and the people with whom you are working. In fact, you might do all of this so subtly that no one would ever know you are doing it! I'll let you use your creativity to adapt these ideas to your specific situations.

About the Exercises

The following two exercises will help you get in touch with your momentary dreaming substyle while working. In the first exercise, you'll explore visual flirts. In the second, you'll have the chance to notice and follow subtle movement tendencies. Again, I'd like to give you the freedom to take the time and space to unfold these experiences in a much fuller way than you might do when you are actually working with people. If you want, you could go much further and express your experiences through painting, dance, music, or whatever creative modality you choose. At the end of the exercises, take time to recall what you learned about your momentary dreaming substyle, and how these experiences might even accompany or enhance the learned skills you already know.

As always, do these exercises with a partner or alone, imagining a client or group with which you work. And please alter the exercise to fit your situation (coach, facilitator, teacher, etc.). I will describe the exercise as if you were working as a therapist with someone else. If you do work with a "real" person, once again, the *focus is on you, the therapist/facilitator.*

How Flirts and Your Momentary Dreaming Process Show the Way

(One person is the "therapist," one is the "client.")

1. To the person working as the therapist: describe your ordinary/primary substyle of working.

2. Now relax your mind, your eyes; let yourself become a bit dreamy, and look around and notice something that quickly catches your attention. If there are a few things, let your dreamy mind choose one on which to focus. Meditate on that flirt. What was it about it, that caught your attention (its color, shape, feeling, quality, etc.)?

3. Now, *become* this flirt, in some way. That is, feel it in your body, take its form or posture, make its gestures or motions, and let it inform you about the momentary dreaming substyle it is suggesting for your work. Also notice any possible information from the "field" that it may be bringing to you about your work with your client.

4. Now, therapist, please try to use this substyle as you begin to work with your client, for a few minutes.

That is, stay close to its quality and let it inform your work in some way.

5. Afterwards, notice and speak about how this style affected your work and what you learned. Then get feedback from your client.

You can also adapt this exercise in the following way:

Begin to work with someone, and then, when you experience a moment of confusion or feel a bit unknowing, let yourself become a bit dreamy. Then, look around with foggy eyes and catch and unfold a flirt, as above. Sense what this flirt is expressing, how it might inform your style, and how it might add new information about the situation. Then, use this new style in some way, to continue to work on the situation with your client.

How Movement Tendencies Can Express your Momentary Dreaming Process

One of my all-time favorite exercises that Arny developed many years ago, and that I go back to, again and again, involves following movement flirts; that is, following the subtlest movement tendencies that occur in your body. Movement tendencies occur at the flirt level, but are simultaneously very close to the Essence Level, as you will see in some of the next chapters. In this exercise, you will focus on the slightest movement tendency that occurs in your body while you are working and the momentary dreaming substyle it is suggesting.[64]

Slight movement tendencies are different from double signals. They are so subtle and fleeting that they may not yet be perceptible on the outside. For example, your head might move slightly to the right, yet, it is so subtle that it can't be seen on the outside.

Let me first give you an example. A student in one of my classes was working with a partner. She was intent on noticing the structure of what was happening with her partner/client and following this person's signals. At one point while working, she noticed a slight tendency for her torso to lean to the side. She unfolded this experience and had the feeling that her body would like to lie down. She imagined lying down and realized that this suggested a more relaxed and easy-going style for her work. She told her client that she needed to pause for a moment, relax, and go very slowly. Her client was thrilled, because he wanted to

do that, too, but felt that he had never had the permission to actually slow down.

As this example shows (and as I have been suggesting), an unexpected result of following flirts can reveal not only an important momentary dreaming substyle that wants to emerge in a given moment, but often brings information that directly connects to your client's process, as well. You'll remember how Jung's memory of a song his mother sang connected deeply with his client. Arny has said that at this flirt level, experiences are *nonlocal,* in the sense that they do not belong just to you or the client, but to the larger field of which you are a part. In a recent class, he said, "If you want to get along with somebody else, go deeply into yourself. If you are deep in yourself, you will connect better with others." (I will refer to nonlocality in the next chapters on your deep essence substyle.)

The exercise can be done rapidly, and in fact, I think it works best as a training exercise if you do it in just 10 minutes, or so. Once again, I will write this exercise as if you are working with someone else, but you can also do it internally, by imagining that you are working with someone (or a couple or group). Again, the focus is on your development as facilitator. Both you and your "client" will give you the permission to temporarily interrupt the flow of your work together, in order to focus on, explore, and unfold one of your movement tendencies. You'll then let that information influence your style and see how it affects your work with your partner.

Movement Tendencies and your Momentary Dreaming Substyle

1. One person is the client, one the therapist. The therapist works with the client for a few minutes.

2. Then, therapist, please excuse yourself for a couple of minutes, to do the following innerwork *silently*:

   • Relax, close your eyes, and take a couple of breaths. Let your mind become unfocused, for a moment.

   • Focus on your body and notice where your body is *tending to move,* just now. *Don't move yet;* just notice a tendency for your body to move in a particular way or direction.

   • Now, let that subtle motion begin to unfold throughout your body. Allow images and possibly sounds to emerge that go along with that experience and continue until you have a sense of what this subtle movement is trying to express.

- Make a note about what you discovered and write down a line or two of poetry to capture that experience. When you are ready, sense the momentary dreaming substyle this experience is suggesting.

3. Now, as you return to working with your client, try to use this dreaming substyle for a few minutes, in some way that feels right for you. Please use your awareness of feedback to notice what is happening with your client, and also, use any other skills, as needed.

4. Then, discuss:

- How did your movement experience influence your style? What effect did this have on your client, and her or his process? Did your experiences connect in some way to your client's process?

- How might you experiment and enjoy dreaming and lucidity more, in your everyday life?

Examples of the Exercise

I remember a coach who felt a slight movement tendency, in which his shoulders and head began to sink downwards. As he followed that tendency in his body, he suddenly had the image of a frog sitting and croaking near a pond. The frog was relaxed and simply breathing, and then, would suddenly jump up and catch a fly in its mouth! As a coach, he imagined he would simply be present with his coachee. That is, he would be quiet, grounded, and in touch with the earth and would wait until something caught his attention and then go deeply into it. This was very different than his primary style that was very attentive, upbeat, and quick-paced![65]

Relaxed Frog (iclipart image)

Here is one final example, that happened during a supervision session I did with a therapist. The therapist described a situation with one of her clients who was having numerous relationship issues. She had tried to help the client find resolutions to those relationship problems, but nothing seemed to help. In fact, the therapist was puzzled why this client even came back to therapy!

After discussing the issue, I asked the therapist to experiment with following her sentient movement tendencies. She noticed her head moving slightly downward and her chest receding. She unfolded this experience and went even further down and inward. She then realized that she needed this state very badly: that is, being deep inside herself and trusting her own feelings and wisdom. What momentary dreaming facilitator substyle would this create? She said this would create a style in which she would stay close to her own inner depths. When she imagined using this style with this client, she was very surprised. She said that she, the therapist, would talk more about herself! That is, she would tell this client how she has similar problems to the client, and she would also speak about how she, herself, resolves these problems in her own life.

The therapist then had an insight. She realized that while she had been focusing on helping her client *solve* her relationship problems, in actuality, her client needed to learn more about the *process of relating*. The therapist then knew that this was why the client kept coming back to therapy! That client was seeking to learn more about *how to relate to others*. Instead of focusing on finding solutions, the therapist needed to help the client focus on the *details of relating*. This was helpful to that therapist, and ultimately, to the client, as well.

As you can see, opening up to the information embedded within momentary flirts, whether from inside you, or the field around you, can bring insightful information for your work and help you connect more deeply to those with whom you work.

Now, let's begin to explore your deep substyle.

CHAPTER 14
Deep Substyle

I TRIED MANY TIMES *to write this chapter while sitting in front of my computer, but was not successful. I took a break, had a good discussion with Arny about the Essence Level, and then stole another few minutes to play my piano, before returning to my writing.*

As my fingers touched the piano keys, I began to relax. I found myself humming and rocking back and forth on my seat as I played, enjoying the melody and a sense of spaciousness in the field around me. When I returned to my computer, the thoughts that had previously been jumbled in my head began to flow in a clearer way. I realized that I had just connected to the Essence Level and could now write about it, and our deep substyle, more easily.

As you can imagine, your deep substyle grows out of the Essence Level (which you see in the Deep Democracy diagram below). You'll remember that the Essence Level refers to the most subtle and sentient experiences you have, which can almost not be spoken, and the experience of being moved by the earth and the universe around you. As Essence Level experiences begin to unfold further into awareness, they emerge first in terms of Flirts, then images in Dreamland, and finally in words that can be spoken in Consensus Reality.

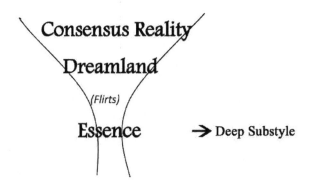

You had a brief taste of the Essence Level in the exercise on movement tendencies in the preceding chapter. While following a slight movement tendency (or flirt) in your body, you may have noticed a subtle *force* or *field power* that seems to move you about. It is like the gravity field that pulls you but cannot be seen directly. Arny called the intelligence and organizing power behind this subtle force or power the *Processmind* (which we'll explore in Chapter 19).

Each of us has had a sense of the Essence Level. Perhaps it has emerged spontaneously during moments when you have connected with special spots on the earth, or have felt moved by the universe around you. At other times, aspects of your deep essence substyle have appeared when you were a child, or through the behavior of someone who was very important to you in life. I'll draw on some of these experiences, and more, in the next section and explore how to more consciously bring the qualities these experiences engender into your work.

When you are close to the Essence Level, there is a sense of *oneness* in which you are no longer split between all of the various *parts* within you, but rather, you touch on something more fundamental. In other words, the Essence Level is like the ground from which all your individual and separable parts and figures arise. It includes, but is greater than, all of them.

Your Deep Substyle

As a facilitator, when you are in touch with the Essence Level, it creates your deep substyle. In those moments, you can sense a kind of openness and a feeling of eldership, in which you are able to embrace and flow with your own parts and experiences, as well as those of the individual or groups with which you work. This openness also makes it possible to let go of your everyday mind and open up to new insights and creativity for your work. Most facilitators have said that when they are in touch with this substyle, they have the feeling that they don't have to *try* to do the methods they have learned; rather, those methods seem to arise fluidly, on their own.

You will also sense that your deep substyle is the ground from which all your other substyles emerge. In other words, it contains each of them, yet is greater than their sum. Most importantly, the very individual way that the Essence Level expresses itself through you will be colored and shaped by your unique nature.

So, Why Do I Need Other Substyles?

I can imagine that you might be saying, "Hey, if the deep substyle is so wonderful and encompassing, why not just stay close to it and forget everything else?" Well, you have a good point!

However, it would not be natural! Sometimes, you are closer to your primary substyle and identity, or your secondary substyle. There is a natural flow within you between all substyles. Each one is valuable and seeks expression, and *together*, they make up the unique gifts you bring to your work and to your life.

A deeply democratic attitude would embrace all parts and substyles within you, knowing that each one is a natural and important part of your artist's palette. In fact, as you'll see in Part V, each substyle is central to a larger mythic pattern and story that flows throughout your life and work.

However, I do want to say that if you lose access to this deep substyle over long periods of time, you'll tend to burn out. Appreciate your primary, secondary, and momentary substyles, and then, when you feel inhibited or sense that something is missing from your work, you can once again seek the deep essence substyle that moves you.

The Many Facets of Your Deep Substyle

Since your deep essence substyle arises out of the most sentient and subtle experiences that can hardly be spoken about, any *one* description will not be enough to fully grasp it. At best, descriptions merely point toward these immeasurable experiences. Therefore, I devoted all of Part IV to a number of exercises to facilitate your experience of your deep substyle from different angles. At the end of Chapter 20, you'll have a chance to intuit the basic or unifying spirit behind all of them.

The Cubist Facilitator

A Short Vignette

I COULDN'T HELP BUT *include this little vignette, before going on to Part IV!*

I realized the other day that the art of Cubism, which I have been studying recently, provides a wonderful analogy to the way in which our many substyles add up to our unique facilitator style.

Cubism was created by Pablo Picasso and George Braque, in the early 20th century. Cubist artists believed that you can only truly understand something if you view it from many angles, simultaneously. In the same way, you can only truly grasp your unique style and your art as a facilitator by sensing and knowing *all of the substyles* that comprise it. When put together, they add up to the rich complexity of your unique facilitator style.

Your facilitator substyles are sometimes quite contradictory! For example, your primary substyle is most often *very different* from your secondary substyle. If you were to make a drawing of yourself that included all of your substyles in one portrait, it might end up looking like a Cubist painting! In fact, you might try that! One substyle (or eyeball or part of your body) might be looking in one direction, while another substyle (eyeball or part of the body) might be turned in an utterly different direction!

I was delighted to learn that the physicist, Niels Bohr, also drew from Cubist thinking to explain the properties of an electron, which has, simultaneously, properties of both particles and waves. Apparently, " . . . Bohr used not a scientific figure, but a Cubist painting in his house. He told his students that to fully understand something you have to see it from many different perspectives that might first appear to contradict each other—just as a Cubist painter depicts a figure from multiple angles at once."[66]

In the same way, I hope you will embrace the nature of your various facilitator substyles, imagining them as the sometimes contradictory, yet complementary, colors, shapes, and angles that together make up your art and your most special way of facilitating!

PART IV
Exploring Facets of Your Deep Substyle

CHAPTER 15

The Deep Substyle Exercises

IN THIS SECTION, you will have the chance to explore your deep substyle from many different angles, and the special way the Essence Level expresses itself through your unique nature. As I mentioned in the last chapter, because this style *can't quite be said,* there is no *one* description or exercise that will suffice to get in touch with its nature. That is, there are innumerable ways to sense and describe its subtle and sentient power. Just as you might describe the ocean as deep, vast, blue, flowing, powerful, splashing, etc., your deep substyle can only be grasped by experiencing and describing it from various angles, all of which add up to its fundamental nature.

When you are in touch with this substyle, it often feels like coming "home." Some of my students called it the "sweet spot" or "being in the zone." It can also bring a more fluid, easy, and creative access to your skills. A great paradox, as I have mentioned earlier in the book, is that even if you do not identify with this part of you consciously, people sense it in you. In fact, many are drawn to you just *because of* this quality.

When you are close to your deep substyle, it often gives you the feeling of not having to *try* to do the methods you have learned; but rather, they seem to flow more easily out of this deep part of you. In fact, being close to this part of you can help you regain access to your skills, especially when you are under severe tension or stress.[67] Your deep substyle is a centering point and a great inner teacher. If you ever feel lost or in need of help, ask it for guidance.

The Ten-Minute Break Style

You had a taste of one facet of this substyle in Chapter 3, "The Ten-Minute Break Experiment," in which you imagined that you had an unexpected break in the day. I suggested that you could do anything you wanted during those ten minutes that would make you feel well—some activity that you had longed for and perhaps have done for many years. Since this experience is something you are drawn to, something that deeply calls to you, or compels you, over time, it emanates from your deepest Essence Level experience. Therefore, it reveals one facet or quality of the deep substyle behind your work. Take a moment to recall that experience now, or review the notes you wrote down about it.

The Exercises

In the next chapters, I offer a few of the many ways I have used in my classes, to help participants access and experience aspects of their deep Essence Level substyle. Though the exercises are quite different, as you progress through them, you will probably begin to sense how the various experiences of your deep substyle are connected. I will give you the opportunity, in the last chapter, to sense the common thread between them.

The chapters flow between experiences such as adding up your primary and secondary substyles and remembering a unique quality you had as a child. In addition, since the Essence Level is also intimately connected with the natural world around you, you'll have a chance to sense aspects of your deep substyle emerging through the power and feeling of the earth and universe. You may discover that you prefer one method over others, or that you have another method that you tend to use, to get in contact with this part of you. As you progress through the exercises, you will probably sense that this part of you has always been in the background of your work, but you may have gotten out of contact with it.

In my classes, I have found that, in order to get a full sense of these almost ineffable experiences, it is helpful to express them through various creative modalities. Therefore, I sometimes ask you to personify your experience in terms of a mythic or fairytale-like figure, in the form of a drawing, mask, or portrait, and even to put on some makeshift "clothing" to represent and ground your experiences!

Most importantly, please know that the point is not to succeed in the exercises and *do a good job*. Rather, the point is to *give yourself the time and luxury to explore the many facets* of your deep substyle, how you might bring these more fully into your work, and discover the gifts of this level of your facilitation. And, as I mentioned in Chapter 13 on your momentary dreaming style, Arny has said that when you are in touch with your deepest self and follow your most subtle experiences, you may connect to those with whom you work, in a profound and nonlocal way.

Progress through the chapters in a linear way, or choose the chapters that "flirt" with you in the moment. Please be sure to make notes about your experiences. As always, the way in which you bring these experiences into practice depends entirely upon your feelings, the special moment and time, and the person with whom you are working. Finally, please know that while the following exercises are geared toward enriching your work with others, they are ultimately meant to inspire you to bring this level more fully into your life as a whole.

Mild Chronic Depression

Before beginning the exercises, I want to mention one of the central reasons it is important to have access to the Essence Level and your deepest substyle. If you are not in touch with it, you might experience something that Arny calls a *mild chronic depression* (as mentioned in Chapter 4). In contrast to a serious depression, a mild chronic depression is a subtle background feeling in which you feel that life is just OK; that is, you can function and do your work, but you sense that something is basically missing. You don't have much motivation or passion for what you are doing. You might feel uninspired, lethargic, or even bored. Getting back in touch with your deep substyle can re-inspire you and remind you of the fundamental motivation and passion that move you and all you do.[68]

OK, let's begin to explore some of the facets of your deep substyle. Then, in the final fifth section of the book, we'll begin gathering all of your substyles together, to discover how they are patterned in early dreams and how, together, they form your unique and mythic facilitator "dance."

CHAPTER 16
Adding Up and Wearing Your Substyles

*T*HERE ARE MANY *ways to get in touch with facets of your deep substyle. In this chapter, you'll have the chance to explore a simple method in which you will literally "add up" two of your substyles, to discover the deep substyle in the background. This experience will also bring together some of the other experiences you have had, in earlier exercises.*

As I said in earlier chapters, your deep substyle is the sum of all of your substyles, and yet, is greater than that sum. In this simple exercise, you will have the chance to explore *adding up* your substyles. For simplicity, I will ask you to focus on your primary and secondary substyles. You'll let your hands represent each of these substyles and then sense the way they come together. This summation will reveal an aspect of your deep essence substyle. I'll then ask you to *wear* this substyle! Wear it? Yes! If you can, please find something to put on to help you feel that deep substyle. You might put a scarf over your head, a coat or sheet around you, etc. I have found that literally *wearing it* can give you a deeper feeling of that special way of facilitating!

You will need a few pieces of paper, something to write with, and if possible, colored markers to make notes and sketches. I have put some pictures next to the steps of the exercises, to illustrate one of my supervisee's experiences of the various steps. Afterwards, I will speak more about their experience.

Adding Your Primary and Secondary Substyles and Wearing Your Deep Nature

1. Recall your ordinary or primary substyle when working with people, facilitating, teaching, etc. (for

example, kind, related, firm, direct). Express the quality, feeling, energy, and rhythm of this style with the motions of one of your hands (for example, strong, gentle, slow, fast). Make a little sketch in some way on your paper to represent this style and quality, and add some words to describe this primary substyle.

*Open and Embracing
Primary Substyle*

2. Now, do the same thing for your secondary style. To do this, recall an aspect of your secondary substyle that you explored previously, in the book. Or imagine that you were working with someone and could be totally free. What secondary or anti-style would emerge (for

*Firm and Direct
Secondary Substyle*

example, detached, direct, exact, psychic)? Express the quality, feeling, energy, and rhythm of that style with your *other* hand. When you are ready, make a little sketch of this substyle and add a couple of words to describe it. Go back and forth, expressing one hand and then the other, until you get a good feeling for both.

3. Now, when you are ready, put your hands down and relax for a moment. That is, relax your mind, take a few breaths, relax your body, and let your eyes

become a bit dreamy and unfocused. Then, let each of your hands, once again, express your primary and secondary substyles. Now, still in this relaxed and slightly dreamy state, let your hands just "*do something*" with each other. That is, let them *find a relationship* or a third "something" together. Let this happen very spontaneously, without effort or thinking. Your hands will know what to do. Wait until a third experience or resolution appears between these processes and energies that are often quite different from one another, even if it seems irrational.

Third Experience or Resolution: One Hand Holding the Other Firmly While the Other Hand Opens Up.

What relationship or resolution did they find? Meditate on this experience and then try to *feel it in your body*. As you do that, sense what this experience is expressing to you. Make a note about it on your paper.

Now, ask yourself, what piece of nature could represent this experience best? (For example, a tree, a mountain, bird, sky, water.) Let this pop up spontaneously, and then, experiment becoming like that piece of nature, yourself. That is, embody it by

standing or sitting like that part of nature, feel it in your body, make its sounds, movements, etc.

Now, imagine that this piece of nature and spot could be represented by some *human-like* figure. What human figure would it be? What does that figure look like? What does its face look like? How does that person stand, and move? What do they wear?

When you are ready, *become this figure* yourself. To do this, look around and grab something like a coat or scarf and put it on or around you to help you feel your way into being that figure. That is, *wear* this aspect of your deep substyle! Take this figure's posture (sitting or standing). Make motions like the figure would make; think her, his or their thoughts; feel what it is like to have that person's body and mind, and imagine speaking like her, him, or them. Take a moment to sense the figure's deep goal or intention in life. Make notes and a little sketch of this figure on your paper.

Woman Deep Within Herself and Open to Spontaneous Feelings and Ideas

4. Now, imagine that this figure (if you haven't already) is a therapist, teacher, coach, or other helper or facilitator! What style would that person have? Imagine the gestures, motions, facial expressions, and posture that go with that style. Take a moment

to act out this person's style, as if she or he or they were working with others. Make notes about this style.

Now, act out this person and her, his, or their style, once again, and as you do that, notice if in some way the imagined person *includes* both your primary and secondary styles, with their qualities, feelings, and energies within it. Make a note about this. Finally, imagine using this style with a client, group, organization, or others with whom you work.

5. Reflect on your experience and make notes about the following questions:

    •   How is this aspect of your deep substyle different from your primary way of working? What was it like, to imagine using it? Did it bring to birth any new types of creativity? Did it somehow include the qualities or energies of your primary and secondary styles?

    •   Can you sense how your learned skills might flow out of this deep substyle, as you are working?

    •   Are you aware of how this deep style is *already present* in the way you work with people? Perhaps it appears first in your double signals, or in deep inner feelings? How has this part of you expressed itself in different parts of your life?

    •   Imagine being in touch with this part of you in your future work. If you are unsure how to do this, ask your deep self-figure this question and wait for its responses. It is your best teacher!

An Example

Here is an example that accompanies the images alongside the exercise. One of the facilitators in my class said that her primary style was being very open to those with whom she works. She showed this with an open hand. Her secondary style was being firm and direct, which she showed with a fist. She noted that this fist was closed and conveyed the quality of being deeply within herself.

When she relaxed, the two hands found a relationship in which the firm hand tightly held the open hand. This experience reminded her of a tree that was firmly rooted in the ground, yet at the same time, had branches that opened up to the sky and moved with the breeze. As a figure, she imagined the tree as a woman who was rooted deeply in herself, yet would respond spontaneously, when things happened around her.

When she imagined using these qualities in her work with people, she experienced them as very freeing. She would be very close to her inner experience and spontaneously bring advice or ideas when they emerged inside of her. It felt, to her, as if she were sitting within her deepest, wisest essence. To embody these qualities and experience their coalescence even more, she tilted her head downward and put a blanket over her head.

She noticed that both her primary and secondary substyles were part of this figure and style, but in a more fluid and integrated way. She was like the closed fist, deep and firmly rooted inside herself, but also open and responsive when impulses emerged spontaneously.

As you may have experienced in the exercise, your deep

substyle is an encompassing experience that contains within it the energies and qualities of your primary and secondary substyles, and yet, is greater than both. When you are in touch with this aspect of your deep substyle, *wear* it and let its wisdom and feelings influence the work that you do.

CHAPTER 17

Your Unique Child Style

*The most sophisticated people I've ever known
had just one thing in common: they were all in
touch with their inner children.*[69]

—Jim Henson, U.S. puppeteer and
creator of the Muppets

*I*N THIS CHAPTER, *you'll have the opportunity to discover special qualities of your deep substyle that appeared in your childhood.*

Anyone who knows me knows that I love to play. I especially love to play with puppets and art materials and take every opportunity to get others to play with me, as well!

While writing this part of the chapter, I dreamed that there was a little child on a swing. He wore a soft furry hat and swung his feet forward and backward. In the dream, it was known that this child was a great teacher. In fact, he was *the* great teacher. People came to him to learn and he did what he normally does—that is, play! This was his teaching! When I woke up, I knew that the child part of us is one of our best teachers, bringing special qualities that belong to our deep substyles.

Lately, I've been reading a book about the childhoods of some well-known artists.[70] There was always something quirky, unusual, gifted, or weird about them! I began to think of some of the things I did or felt as a child; qualities that seemed unusual or unique, which have remained in my memory until today. At the same time, some of my clients and supervisees began to spontaneously talk about special characteristics of their childhood behaviors, as well. All of this caused me to research the link between unique childhood qualities and our deep substyles. I also want to say that I have previously written about, and gave an exercise on, the *older part* of us, as an important aspect of our deep substyle. You might check it out, in order to explore the other side of the age spectrum![71]

In any case, I realized that if a particular quality from childhood remains in our memories over time, it must be mythic for us; that is, it is a central part of us that longs for greater awareness.[72] It is still moving us and trying to come not only into our life as a whole, but into our work with others, revealing a special aspect of our deepest facilitator substyle.

When I brought these ideas and the following exercise to my classes, I was thrilled to discover the unusual and quirky aspects of the participants as children, as well as the qualities these childlike experiences suggested for their deep facilitator substyles.

Ask Yourself This Question

To begin, I'd like to ask you to consider a question. However, I'm not sure exactly how to phrase it! So, I will give some hints and trust that your inner wisdom will choose the answer that is right for you.

Basically, I am interested in focusing upon a special part of you that revealed itself when you were a child—that is, a quality, ability, or thing you did that revealed something unique and unusual about you—something that you *had to do, think, or feel,* that *fascinated* you, *drew you* to it, or *compelled you* so much that you just *had to do it,* as a child! For example, you may have felt that you had to be in nature and went there as often as possible. Maybe you had to save animals. Some people said they just had to play an instrument. Others loved making things. Some were constantly creating science experiments. Some told themselves stories about some miraculous fairytale figure, when they were trying to go to sleep.

If you don't remember your childhood, or it was very difficult and you can't remember much, you can go back as far as you can, in your memory. It is also possible that this special quality appears in a memory you were told by *someone else,* about you. Perhaps your parents remembered this particular quality about you, but you don't remember it, yourself. If that story has stayed with you over time, then this is fine to explore as well.

Of course, there may be a couple of things that come to mind. All of them are important. In the exercise, I would suggest that you choose the one that comes up strongest in the moment, or the one that occurred earliest in your life. You will discover how this quality or experience reveals a hidden, yet central aspect of your facilitator deep substyle.

Before going further, take a few minutes to think to yourself about this unique part of you from childhood and make a note about its special quality or behavior. (If you are with a group, it can be fun to interview one another about this quality, which you may have never shared before.) That is, think about and discuss a quality, ability, or thing you did as a child, or as early back as you can remember, that revealed something unique and different about you. Perhaps it was something that you *had to do, think, or feel,* that *fascinated* you, *drew* or *compelled* you.

Here are a couple of answers from my class participants. An organizational facilitator who focuses primarily on social issues said that her family was not a very friendly place to grow up. She was surprised to recall a quality in herself that seemed to come out of nowhere (considering her difficult home situation). When her parents put her and her siblings to bed, she would spontaneously begin singing. This created a fun and funny atmosphere, and she and her siblings would then fall asleep, together. When I asked her what it was about singing that was important, she replied, "It creates another reality. Not the ordinary life of quarreling and feeling left out or hurt. It created more connectedness and fun and caring, even though, at that age, I did not have the ordinary language to express those things." She said the singing just *happened to her;* she did not think it out or *try* to be loving. While she was certainly making up for a difficult home life, this quality is also central to who she is and her unique style. And it is behind her deep desire to work with social issues and to care for the world.

Another woman, who is a spiritual healer and teacher, said that as a child she remembers jumping on a cushy chair and standing on her head. Why? She said it was really fun, pleasurable, and turned the world upside down! When the world was upside down, she felt that it became magical; it expanded and became more non-ordinary; it was then possible to experience things you can't experience, otherwise. Actually, this is the world that she lives in and teaches about, and now she wanted to learn to bring this quality even more into her own facilitator style.

As these experiences show, I believe that this quality, ability, feeling, or characteristic is something you were born with, and therefore it is mythic for you; that is, a deep part of you at the Essence Level that was, and will always be, there. You didn't *try to make it happen; it was just YOU*. And it's a key to a special aspect of your unique and deep substyle, even if you're usually not quite in touch with it.

Early Passions

While writing this book, I came across Robert Greene's book, *Mastery,* in which he speaks of something comparable to this idea of recalling what we felt compelled to do as children.[73] Greene talks about an early passion in childhood that is an indication of your life task. He describes it as a powerful force that moves us, like the basic force that turns a seed into a particular flower, and that draws each of us to a certain vocation. He says it points towards what he calls our "primal" uniqueness.[74] Greene says that this early passion has always been there, driving us, but we may try to avoid it and go in a different direction. If we don't follow it, we get listless, bored, or unhappy.

This is reminiscent of Carl Jung's idea that our childhood dream is indicative of the profession we will choose in life. Arny took Jung's interest in childhood dreams further and showed how they are connected to chronic body symptoms and are also indicative of our long-term mythic paths in life. (We'll explore your childhood dream and myths in Part V.)

Greene tells stories of such people as Albert Einstein, John

Coltrane, Marie Curie, and Leonardo da Vinci, who all had powerful experiences that impacted them as children, which moved them to their chosen life task or profession.[75] For example, when Marie Curie, the discoverer of radium, was four, "she wandered into her father's study and stood transfixed before a glass case that contained all kinds of laboratory instruments for chemistry and physics experiments." Apparently, she went back to that room many times, imagining experiments she could do with the tubes and measuring apparatus.[76] The great jazz musician John Coltrane was touched to the core, hearing the unique sounds of Charlie Parker playing saxophone. He felt, at that moment, that music could express his emotional and spiritual longings, which he had not been able to express in words. This was the beginning of his intense practice of the saxophone, which led to him becoming a great jazz musician.[77]

Notes about the Exercise

In the following exercise, you'll have the opportunity to explore a unique quality from childhood and discover how it reveals a special aspect about your facilitator's deep substyle. After unfolding that quality from childhood, I'll ask you to imagine a storybook or mythic figure that represents this part of you. You'll draw this figure, become it, and find out the style it's recommending for your work. Finally, you'll imagine using that (deep) substyle with a client or group. You'll discover the spontaneous creativity it brings to your work and how this substyle dovetails with your learned skills.

Again, I want to give you the freedom to explore your unique style in a relatively uninhibited way, more freely than you might with an actual client. Perhaps you will start to sing, move, dream, meditate, etc. I won't focus on the particulars of how you will, then, actually adapt and integrate this experience and style into your work. I'll leave that up to your creativity.

You will need a pen and paper for notes and possibly a big piece of paper and markers to make a drawing. If you do this exercise with an actual partner, I would recommend that you take about 25 minutes, per person.

Your Unique Child and Deep Substyle Exercise

1. Recall the special quality you thought about earlier, which revealed something unique about you, as a child. Sitting or standing, *imagine* and then *re-feel this special quality again, now,* in your body and mind. Take its posture, make its motions, listen to or make sounds that go with it. As you do that, notice the body feeling this experience creates,

and where you feel centered in your body. Notice how you use your eyes, your posture, your hands, breath, etc. Sense what it is about that experience that is so unique, or special. Write down a few key words that capture the essence of that experience for you.

2. Embody that experience, once again, and now *exaggerate* or *amplify* it a bit, in some way. That is, do it a bit stronger; fill it out more fully, with more movement, sound, feeling, etc. And as you do that, imagine that you are not just *you*, but that you are some *real or mythic figure,* who is moving and acting this way. What kind of figure are you? Speak a little bit, as this figure. Who are you? What do you do? Where are you from? Feel the qualities and feelings that this figure holds. When you are ready, make a sketch of this figure (on your big paper), give it a name, and make a few notes about it, and its qualities. Perhaps your drawing will give you even more insight into that figure, in some way.

3. Finally, re-feel this figure once again, embody/ become it, and now *sense the style* it would have or suggest, for working with others as a therapist or facilitator. Imagine using this style with your clients (or with whomever you work). Make notes.

4. Now, imagine (or try with a partner) using that style with a client (or coachee, student, organization, etc.). Notice how this style *spontaneously develops its own creative methods.* Feel free to also bring in, and flow with, any of your other substyles and any of your learned skills, if they arise.

5. Finally, discuss the following and make notes:

    •   What was it like to use this deep substyle in your
        work? Did any spontaneous creativity or new
        methods emerge? How is this style similar to,
        or different from, your primary and secondary
        substyles?

    •   Are you aware of how this deep style/experience
        has *already appeared*, or *tried to appear,* in your
        work with people (for example, spontaneous
        experiences, fantasies, body symptoms/
        experiences, body signals, etc.)? Also, how has
        it appeared, or tried to appear, in various parts
        of your life?

    •   What does this experience teach you about
        your very unique nature and special way of
        working with others? How might this inform
        your work in the future (and, possibly, your life
        as a whole)?

An Example

A man in my class spoke about being a helper in his father's
grocery store, when he was a young child. At that time, he
said he always felt well if he could simply carry a basket out
to a customer's car. It was a simple act, and he did not expect
anything in return. The figure that he imagined was Mahatma
Gandhi. For him, Gandhi represented a simple, humble, and
beautiful presence. He felt shy about this, but was very moved,
and sensed how these unique qualities could deeply influence
his work with others. He described this quality as "simple
presence," with which he would identify, and manifest in
his work. He realized that this experience resonated with his

current life situation, in which he had gone through some turbulent times, and now, was finding a kind of peace.

An Essential Part of Your Work and Life

My hope, in this exercise, is that you sensed how this special quality from your childhood, which is utterly unique to you, has *always* been in the background of your work. In fact, it has been influencing you throughout your life, moving you and trying to emerge into awareness. You may also have noticed how this unique part of you is connected to many things you have done over your lifetime, but may not have realized. You are born with this force. It is a unique gift that wants to enrich all you do and bring more creativity and wisdom to your work.

I want to stress, again, that the methods you learn are wonderful. Learn them, use them. They are amazing tools. At the same time, you have something utterly unique that you were born with, that wants to use those tools in your own special way.

The way that each of us is propelled in life, by the things that really move us at a young age, reminds me of a quote that Arny once brought to his class from the U.S. theologian and civil rights activist, Howard Thurman. Thurman once said, "Don't ask what the world needs. Ask what makes you come alive, and go do it. Because what the world needs is people who have come alive."[78]

Of course, we should all follow whatever we feel the world needs. Yet, Thurman is reminding us that the basic forces that *bring us to life*—and here I am stressing those things that move us early in life—are needed for our world. Connect with them, follow them. Let them inspire your deep substyle and bring your work to life, in your own inimitable way.

Of course, you will not be connected to this special quality of the *younger you* and the way it informs your deep substyle, all the time. All of your substyles are equally important and arise in various moments while working. At the same time, if you can, at times, connect with this quality—with that which *makes you come alive*—you will manifest something special, with which you were born, to help our little world. It will ensure that your work is impassioned, artistic, full of spirit and heart, and that you feel well and renewed from day to day.

CHAPTER 18

Through the Lens of Special People

Ben Thompson, Antioch College, circa 1980

*I've learned that people will forget what you said,
people will forget what you did,
but people will never forget how you made them feel.*[79]

—Maya Angelou, U.S. poet, author, performer,
and civil rights activist

SOME OF THE *unique qualities that lie behind your deep substyle can be found in people who have been especially influential in your life. In this chapter, you'll have a chance to explore one such person and the way that person reflects central elements of your deepest way of working.*

Many of us have had teachers, advisers or other people who have modeled some special characteristics that resonate with our most basic and deep nature. It could be a teacher that you had many years ago, a special friend, or a mentor. Or it could be someone you just happened to meet one time in your life, and yet that meeting and moment in time had a profound and lasting positive effect on you. You may find yourself telling stories about this special individual, over and over again. Some of these people may have had impressive skills, yet I imagine it was their *unique way of doing things*, their feelings about life, and the way these manifested in their behavior, that remained in your heart.

For example, I remember Arny telling stories about two of his Jungian analysts in Zurich. The way they did Jungian analysis was quite different from the traditional model. One of them, Barbara Hannah, was very spontaneous. Franz Riklin, who was C. G. Jung's nephew, whom I mentioned in a previous chapter, didn't interpret Arny's dreams (dreams being a cornerstone of Jungian analysis)! Rather, Riklin was very shamanic and talked a lot about *himself* during *Arny's* sessions with him! Arny loved both of these analysts and learned a great deal from them about himself, even though they didn't do Jungian work in a traditional way. As I mentioned earlier in the book, I have always been curious why people laugh and are so delighted when Arny tells stories about them in his classes. It is something about Hannah's and Riklin's unique ways of working with, and living, the unconscious that seem to bring a sense of freedom and a world of possibilities.

One of My Teachers

Let me tell you about one such person in my own life. In the late 1970s and early 80s, when I was at Antioch College in Ohio, one of my most inspiring teachers was Ben Thompson—to whom I am deeply indebted for introducing me (and many of my friends) to Arny! Ben gave classes in the education department, one of which was called "The Learner and the Learning Process." I loved that class, and I loved Ben as a teacher. His inimitable style interrupted all preconceptions that I had had about how a teacher should behave!

More often than not, Ben entered the classroom without knowing exactly what he was going to do. He appeared completely absorbed in his own inner thoughts. Sometimes he would walk to a particular corner in the classroom, where he would sit down with a treasured book or manuscript that had recently grabbed his attention. With his head tipped downwards in deep contemplation, he would read quietly *to himself,* as we all fidgeted, waiting for him to begin the class! Then, at some unpredictable moment, he would begin to read out loud.

Before I had met Arny, I still remember Ben reading from Arny's earliest manuscript which was called, *The Death Walk.* Arny subsequently updated and published this book under the title, *The Shaman's Body.*[80] (Arny and Ben had met some years earlier. Ben had been one of Arny's PhD teachers.) Completely immersed, Ben read to us with a deep, slow, and impassioned voice. It felt as though he savored and almost breathed in every word. In one particular passage, Arny spoke about the figure of Don Juan from the books of Carlos Castaneda.[81] The section was about the "deathwalk," in which a warrior must walk in front of her or his peers who want to shoot the warrior down, for breaking the rules of the community. The warrior either is shot and dies, or survives the "deathwalk," depending on her or his inner centeredness.

As Ben slowly read Arny's words, I could feel that something moved him far beyond that moment in time and space, and I felt transported as well. I knew that the idea of a "deathwalk" was something deeply meaningful and personal for Ben. In fact, it was so important to him that, as Arny reports in the beginning of *The Shaman's Body*,[82] Ben read the deathwalk chapter onto a tape recorder and asked his wife to play it back at his own funeral. She did so, when he died, some years later.

Another astounding aspect of Ben's teachings, for me, had to do with the requirements for his class. Actually, there was only *one* requirement. He told us that in order to pass the class, we had to *write ten pages. About what?* Ben replied, "*About anything!*" That's right, there were no other guidelines! In fact, we did not even have to attend class, at all! However, he insisted that each of us write those ten pages and put them on his desk before the end of the term, or we would flunk.

This was definitely the first (and probably the last) time I have encountered such an unusual class requirement! I was astonished, shocked, and exhilarated, all at the same time. What could I possibly put on those pages? Well, the material that poured out of me for that "assignment" turned into ten of the most important pages I have ever written in my life. I filled them with stories and feelings from my past that, until that time, I had not dared put into words. My admiration and trust of Ben's radical approach, and what I perceived as a great depth of understanding for all types of experiences, opened a deeply meaningful and new chapter in my own life.

Important People in Your Life

I'd like you to take a moment, now, and think of one such person who was especially influential for you. Think of someone whose unique style of life, or way of working, impressed you so much that it has stayed with you over time. This is probably someone who had a special way of being and navigating through life and the world. Perhaps it was a friend, an old teacher, a mentor, a relative, or simply someone on the street who grabbed your attention and has never drifted from your memory.

Consider what it was about that person that touched you. What qualities did she or he show, that were so important for you? For example, Ben's *way of being* expressed a kind of freedom, for me, about how to live in the world and how to be a teacher.

If this person remains in your memory over a long period of time, her or his way of being is a reflection of particular aspects of your deepest nature and substyle.

The Exercise

Let's explore one of those unique people/teachers in your life. You'll have the chance to step into her or his world and discover the aspect of your deep substyle that is suggested by her or his way of being.

Again, please adapt this exercise to the kind of work you do, whether it be therapy, coaching, facilitation, teaching, etc. You will need paper and a pen or colored markers to make notes and draw a picture.

Finding Your Deep Style through the Lens of Special People in Life

1. Describe your ordinary, primary substyle of working with others.

2. Recall a person/teacher and moment in your life that had a very important and positive effect on you, which has stayed with you for a long time. Who was that person? What was she or he like? Where did you meet this person—or from where did you already know her or him? What place and context? What was it about this person and that moment in time that were so powerful, for you?

3. Now, remember the way that person/teacher behaved at that time. How did she or he speak, act, and move? When you are ready, *shapeshift* into that person. That is, become this special person as you take her or his posture, as you move, speak, and feel your way into that person. Notice how you use your eyes, your posture, your body, your voice, etc.

4. And when you have a good feeling for the qualities of this person, *exaggerate* those qualities and her or his behavior a bit, and imagine that you are not just that person as you knew her or him, but that you are now some *mythic or fairytale figure* who acts in this way! When you have done this, become that figure yourself and imagine you are in some special environment or context. Where are you? What are you doing there? Take a piece of paper and make a drawing of that figure and environment, in some simple way. Then, let a quick story emerge about that figure and environment. Make a note about

that story and sense the learning it is trying to bring you.

5. Now, shapeshift once again, into this mythic or fairytale figure and sense the aspect of your deep substyle that this figure is suggesting for your work with others. Finally, imagine using this style to work with a client, student, group, organization, patient, etc.

6. To finish, ponder the following and make notes.

   - What did this important person and associated mythic figure teach you about your deep substyle?

   - How did you imagine using this deep substyle in practice? In what way would it influence your work and your sense of creativity? Did you imagine that it would use any of your learned skills?

   - In what way have you known this part of you, in various stages or moments in your life?

Those people whom we remember over time, and who have been a strong influence on us, carry some of the unique qualities of our deep substyle as facilitators. Cherish those people and the deep qualities they are suggesting for your work with others.

CHAPTER 19

Your Processmind Earth, Style, and Portrait

*If the sight of the blue skies fills you with joy,
if a blade of grass springing up in the fields
has power to move you, if the simple things of
nature have a message that you understand,
rejoice, for your soul is alive.*[83]

—Eleonora Duse, Italian actor

*I*N THIS CHAPTER, *you'll have a chance to discover and explore aspects of your deep substyle reflected in special spots on the earth.*

From the rolling and crashing waves on the beach, to the vast views from high mountain peaks, from bustling city streets to the arid expanses of the desert, each of us is drawn to particular spots on the earth. These places seem to call to us and reflect our deepest Essence Level natures. When we are there, they are often experienced as wisdom centers and places of greater detachment. Most importantly, they emanate special qualities and energies that are central to our deepest facilitator substyles.

In this chapter, you will have a chance to get in touch with one earth spot that is important for you and discover the special qualities and powers it brings to your deep substyle. You'll then create a mask or portrait that represents the spirit behind that location and these special qualities. I have had a wonderful time introducing this exercise and the creation of portraits with my students. Many of them have kept their portraits or masks for a long time and put them up on their home or office walls, to remind them of their deepest substyle.

The Processmind

In order to understand more about the importance of earth spots, let me tell you a little about Arny's concept of the *Processmind*.[84] Arny defined the Processmind as a subtle and creative intelligence, organizing our spontaneous experiences, such as momentary flirts and dreams. Einstein would have probably understood the Processmind as the "mind of god." The Taoists might call it the "Tao that can't be said."

Again, you may recall the experience you had in the exercise at the end of Chapter 13, on your momentary dreaming substyle. There, you were in touch with the way your body was subtly moved in a particular direction. The Processmind is the creative force and intelligence at the Essence Level that knows how and when to move you in a particular direction. When you're in touch with it, the Processmind often brings insights and approaches to life problems that you may not have been able to imagine from your ordinary state of consciousness. When in touch with it, it also holds the feelings associated with a generous elder who is able to embrace and flow with your own parts and experiences, as well as those of the people with whom you work.

The Processmind and the Earth

Earth spots are one way that the Processmind manifests in our physical realm. When you are near a special earth spot that your deepest self is attracted to, you sense a kind of wisdom and field power all around it. Like many indigenous people around the world, earth spots also have guardian or totem spirits who inhabit and protect them. You might remember the goddess Kannon, of whom I spoke in the Preface. Kannon was fished out of the Senso-ji River and was the enlivening spirit behind the building of the Senso-ji Temple.[85]

When you allow yourself to sense, and be moved by, the powers of a particular earth location that calls to you, the slightly altered state you experience often brings new and illuminating ways of dealing with life's situations that you may not have imagined, from your ordinary state of mind. In turn, the Processmind earth spot also brings some of the most basic and important essence qualities to your deepest facilitator substyle. I notice, when I am in touch with the Processmind and the field-like wisdom behind earth spots as I work, that there is a welcome shift in all I do. My focus turns not only toward the world of *people* and *things,* which is obviously important, but my awareness expands to include the power of nature. I feel that I am not simply *doing* therapy or facilitation, but, rather, I am more in touch with *the way the earth and larger field moves me.* In a sense, when any of us is in touch with the powers of the earth, we *become* nature. As the author, D. T. Suzuki, said, we become like the "showers coming down from the sky . . . like the waves rolling on the beach." In fact we *are* "the showers, the ocean, the stars, the foliage . . ." When this happens, he says, a person becomes a Zen artist in life.[86]

About the Exercise

In the exercise, you will have the opportunity to experience the creative power of the Processmind and an earth spot, and how these illuminate and give birth to central qualities of your deep substyle.[87] You will then have the opportunity to make a creative portrait or mask that represents this spot and your deep substyle.

Let me first introduce you to some of the steps in this three-part exercise. In Part I, you'll get in touch with your Processmind experience in your body and in the earth. You will also recall your primary and secondary substyles and, in the end of the exercise, see how they may be found within your deep facilitator substyle. (You'll recall that your deep substyle includes, yet is larger than, all of your other substyles.)

Then, you will find a place in your body where you sense the deepest and most profound part of you. This step is purely intuitive. Just let your body show you where your deep essence self is located in your body, in the moment. You might sense it in your stomach, your chest, behind your neck, in back of your eyes, in your feet, deep in your solar plexus, etc. You'll then associate that place in your body with a special spot on the earth, and imagine that you go there.

After unfolding your experience of the power, wisdom, and movement of that earth location, I will ask you to imagine that an *earth spirit* arises out of that spot. You'll then unfold this figure further and discover the deep substyle it is suggesting for working with others.

In Part II, you'll have the opportunity to create a portrait or mask of that earth spirit! I will give you three different methods to do this, or you can make up your own. You can simply draw the image on a piece of paper. Or you might gather some colored construction paper, scissors, tape, and markers, to make a mask. A third option is to make a special portrait using colorful chalk pastels, a white oil pastel, and a large piece of black construction paper. Whatever method you choose, I hope you will put this mask/portrait up on your wall, to remind you of it! You'll also need a piece of paper and a pen, to make notes throughout the exercise.

Here is a brief note about the pastel portrait. This method was inspired by the wonderful art of Sandra Silberzweig, which I happened to discover while creating one of my deep substyle classes.[88] From what I understand, Silberzweig is very much at the Essence Level when she paints. She says that she is a "synesthete," meaning that her sensory-grounded channels are so mixed together, they can't be pulled apart. This inseparability is an indication of the Essence Level.

As I researched her work, I stumbled upon a method that many elementary school teachers have used around the world, which is inspired by Silberzweig's pastel drawings. I was so impressed by the amazing and colorful portraits the children made that I just had to try it in my classes![89] In fact, I personally got a little addicted to this method and have made many portraits, over time! In any case, I'll describe parts of the method below, but you can simply use these ideas as a springboard for creating your portrait in any way you like.

Most importantly, in Part III, you'll have the chance to explore how your mask/earth spirit and its qualities would inform and influence your facilitator's deep substyle.

The exercise can be done alone. It is also fun to do with a partner or a group, because you can then share your portraits and learning with each other.

Your Facilitator's Deep Substyle and Portrait Exercise

Part I: The Spirit of the Place

1. Recall/imagine yourself working as a therapist, facilitator, teacher, organizational leader, or however you define what you do. What is your ordinary or primary substyle like? Act out this substyle a little bit and notice what you do with your body, your face, your hands, your posture. Make a little sketch of this style and its type of *energy* in some way, on your paper and write a few words to describe it.

2. Now, recall your secondary substyle, which is further from your awareness and that you "found" in Chapter 12. Or, imagine yourself working with a client as you ordinarily do, and ask yourself, "If I were free, what other style would arise?" (for example, going deep inside, being more direct, being dreamier). Act out this style a little bit and notice how you use your body, face, hands, and posture. Make a sketch of this style and its type of *energy* on your paper and write a few words to describe it. Put your paper to the side.

3. Now, stand if you can (or do this from a sitting position if you can't stand easily) and feel your body. Move a little bit, in place, and scan your body from your head to your feet. As you do that, ask yourself where you sense the deepest part of yourself in your body, just now. That is, where do you sense your deepest self is located in your body? This is an intuitive question. Feel your body and let it spontaneously give you an answer (for example,

is it in your chest, forehead, hips, feet?). When you have found that spot, use your breath to *breathe into* that body area, and notice any movements, sounds, or images that come from that spot.

Wait until you feel that area of your body deeply, and then ask yourself, "What spot on earth would be most closely associated with that deep self-experience?" For example, it might be in the mountains, by the sea, in a forest, by a river, or right in the middle of a city. Choose one.

4. When you have found that earth spot, imagine that you go there. Feel yourself in that spot. Use your breath to breathe into it, as you sense that earth location more deeply. As you do that, begin to sense the whole area and atmosphere around it. Still breathing into that earth area, let the power of that earth spot begin to move you into a kind of dance. Let sounds emerge and even a song, if it happens. As you dance and sing, notice how this experience feels. Continue until *you sense a kind of intelligence or wisdom feeling, all around you.*

5. Now, still experiencing that Processmind earth spot, imagine that *some kind of spirit of that earth spot* emerges out of that land, to be with you; that is, some spirit or figure that represents that earth spot, atmosphere, and your dance. This figure can take on any form; it might be an animal, human, or some other (real or imaginary) nature being. Take your time, until a figure appears spontaneously. What type of earth spirit came out of the land? What quality or energy does it have? How does it move? What does it look like? What kind of face,

body, colors, does it have? Imagine its sounds or voice. Imagine it speaking to you; what does it want to say?

When you are ready, *become that spirit yourself*. Feel it in your body, assume its posture, and let it move you. Let it create its own special dance and make its own sounds/tones or song. As you continue to express that spirit, *imagine the deep style it is suggesting* to you, for working with others. What deep facilitator style is this figure recommending? When you know the style it is recommending, feel it in your body and begin to act it out. Imagine using this style in your work. What is it like to have this style? How do you act, speak, feel, and move? Make notes. Finally, act out that style once more, and notice how it might incorporate the energies of your primary and secondary substyles, in some way. (Look back at your notes if needed.) Make notes.

Part II: Creating Your Deep Substyle Portrait or Mask

6. Staying close to your deep substyle figure and feeling, let yourself drift toward your art materials. Still in touch with the earth figure that arose out of the land, let it represent itself in the form of a deep substyle portrait or mask. That is, let it create a portrait of itself! Choose one of the following three methods.

    • *Simple Mask Drawing.* Draw your spirit-figure's face simply on a piece of paper (or if you want, draw the whole body). Put holes in the area of the eyes so you can see through it. Then hold it up to your face like a mask. Become this figure, feel it, sense it, and when you are ready, give your figure a name and write it down on the back of the mask.

- *Colored Paper Mask.* If you would like to make a more elaborate mask with colored construction paper, first cut out a shape for the head. Then cut out different colors and shapes for the features. Draw anything else you want to add with markers, and glue it all together in some way. Put holes in the spots where the eyes are located. If you want, you can also put small holes on each side of the headpiece, then pull string through those holes and tie the mask around your head. Wear your mask, feel it, become it, and then give your figure a name and write it down, on the back of the mask.

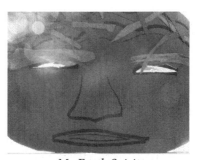

My Earth Spirit
Colored Paper Mask

- *Pastel Portrait.* If you would like to make a pastel portrait, à la Sandra Silberzweig, here are some ideas I learned from one teacher's website.[90] See the examples of my Processmind deep substyle portraits below, and my portrait at the beginning of the vignette called "The Cubist Facilitator" to get an idea about drawing the various lines. You can also use some of the suggestions as a starting point and then continue to fill in your portrait as your impulses and creativity direct. Or just create your portrait in any way you want with pastels, which are really fun to use!

Here is the method: To begin, you will draw lines with a white oil pastel. First draw a U shape for the chin and make lines under it, for the neck. Then, starting from one side of the face, make a candy-cane-shaped nose (or any other shape for a nose). Draw in the other eyebrow and then attach a mouth to the nose and chin with a line. You can draw almond-shaped or another shaped eyes, a line for the lid, and an upside-down rainbow for the iris. You can also use white to color in one part of the eye.

Now, section off parts of the face with lines, color them in any way you like, and add unusual shapes and lines. In general, layer colors of chalk upon other layers to create rich colors. At the end, you might want to trace back over the lines with a white or black oil pastel.

One of my Pastel Portraits

When you are done, put the mask up to your face, feel it, move with it, sense it, and when you are ready, give your figure a name and write it down on the back.

Part III: Unfolding Your Portrait and Deep Substyle

7. Hold your mask in front of your face (or put it on). Sense how it transforms you and step into the deep substyle it is suggesting for your work. Make a simple gesture to capture this style and imagine living it, not only in your work, but also in your life, in general.

8. In what way might this figure and its substyle be mythic for you? That is, how has it appeared in various ways and times, throughout your life?

9. Finally, if you created your portrait with a partner or group, share your experiences. Each hold up your portrait and introduce yourself. Describe and show the gesture of that deep substyle and act it out, a bit. Discuss how that style may incorporate both your primary and secondary substyles. How has this portrait—with its qualities, feelings, and style—manifested, at various times during your life? If you like, try working with a partner for a few minutes, using this deep substyle and exploring its effects on her or him.

An Example

Let me tell you about my own experience. I sensed my deepest self in my chest and heart area and I associated that feeling to a sandy beach on the Oregon coast that I love. I imagined going there. The wind blew strongly through the air and I heard the powerful sounds of the sea. After a while, the wind seemed to blow through me and set me into a flowing dance. The figure that arose was a wind goddess. She was sensitive, deep, inwardly focused, and had a magical power to create new worlds and ideas that would suddenly pop up, and then express themselves intently, in the world.

The style that she suggested was one in which I would be sensitive and attuned to my clients, while also remaining very deeply inside myself, in a kind of dreamy state, sensing the way in which the atmosphere moved me and brought me spontaneous insights. Then, I would trust that these experiences were important to the moment at hand, and creatively bring those insights into the work with my clients. This figure and deep substyle contained the qualities of both my primary substyle

My Processmind Deep Substyle Portrait

of kindness and sensitivity, as well as my secondary style of directness and power. Yet, it was much more than both of them combined. It had a magical and mysterious quality as well. See the picture, "My Processmind Deep Substyle Portrait," that I created. I wish I could reproduce the vibrant pastel colors that I used!

As I meditated on how this style and its qualities have appeared in my life, I recalled my many years of dance training.

I loved to dance, because it often gave me the feeling of flow and being in touch with the powers of the atmosphere. I have also had many powerful experiences of dropping out of consensus reality and gaining spontaneous insights about life. In my musical world, I now see that many of the songs I have written have to do with the power and creativity of the wind, such as one I wrote called, "Let Me Float on the Wind."

In fact, that song brings me to the next chapter, "Spacetime Dreaming Facilitator." Please make sure to put your portrait on your wall to remind yourself of the special and unique qualities that arose out of the earth and helped to bring your deep Essence Level substyle to life.

CHAPTER 20

Spacetime Dreaming Facilitator

*Let me float on the wind like a leaf. Let me land on a
bird's wings, as if it were a reef.
Lift me up in the air so high, throw me towards the
clouds and the sky and then let me float on the wind so
free, who knows what will become of me"*

—From my song, "Let Me Float on the Wind"

A LL OF THE *chapters in this section of the book are focused
on facilitating your experiencing of facets of your deep
substyle. In the last chapter, you discovered an aspect
of this style by getting in touch with the Processmind and its*

connection to special earth spots. In this final chapter in Part IV, I'd like to explore the connection between your deep substyle and your experience of the universe.

Have you ever had the experience of looking up into the sky and imagining what it would be like to float like a leaf or fly like a bird? I have, and I wrote about it in my song *"Let Me Float on the Wind."* Arny calls this experience *spacetime dreaming*.[91] Spacetime dreaming is the natural next step from the Processmind. It expands our attention outward even further from the earth and connects us to the universe all around us. In this chapter, you'll discover the gifts, wisdom, and deep facilitator substyle that arise spontaneously in those moments when you are moved by the cosmos. In order to understand the importance of spacetime dreaming for our work as facilitators, let me tell you a little about it first. It's one of my favorite topics!

Spacetime Dreaming and the "Blurry Space" around You

Arny's concept of spacetime dreaming draws from Albert Einstein's idea about spacetime curvature, which is too complicated to explain, here! But it has to do with the idea that, normally, space seems linear. However, according to Einstein  and his relativity theory, space is *curved*.

We can't see spacetime curvature, but we can sense it moving us, like a field moves a magnetic filing. When we are moved by the universe, it is like entering a subtle essence dreaming field that is blurry, unclear, and noncognitive.

This blurry space, or universal field, seems empty, but many depict and understand it as very full. Take a look at the painting by the 16th-century Japanese painter, Hasegawa Tohaku,[92] of an old painting form called *sumi-e*. In this art form, objects are shown with minimal strokes to capture their essence, and a lot of space is intentionally left blank.

Left panel of the Pine Trees screen by Hasegawa Tohaku
(thanks to Wikipedia)

This "blank" space shows the blurry-foggy power of the field, which in Japanese is called "*Ma.*" It's akin to the "Tao that can't be said." The seemingly blank field is not empty, but rather, full and alive.

As a facilitator, when you let go and get in touch with that blurry space, you begin to sense how the universe moves and guides you. As you open up to this seemingly empty space, Essence Level aspects of your facilitation style can emerge, as well as new spontaneous insights for work. At the same time, you often experience the qualities of an elder who has a sense of detachment and is connected not only with the momentary situation between you and your client(s), but to the field around you and the larger universe.

The Natural Rhythm between Cognitive and Noncognitive Moments

The experience of letting go and being moved by the spaces around you is actually quite well known to all of us, and often sought as a needed state of mind. Arny says that all of us experience aspects of spacetime dreaming when we go to sleep. In addition, many people long for and seek this state, through using addictive substances such as alcohol, drugs, etc. Hopefully, you will be able to use the method in this chapter to access this state in a more useful way, without addictive substances.

Similarly, spacetime dreaming is not only a method to *apply mechanically,* when you are working as a facilitator. In actuality, *all* facilitators go through what I call spontaneous *noncognitive moments.* These moments include those times when you are fatigued, "spaced out," or unable to recall what you have learned.

In Chapter 6, I spoke about those moments when a facilitator loses access to her or his learned skills (when it would otherwise be reasonable to remember them). There are many reasons for this, that I mentioned previously. I also said that behind these difficulties blocking your ability to remember, there is often a hidden gift that wants to be recognized first.

Another basic reason you may, at times, lose access to your skills and linear mindset, is due to the *need to drop out* and gain new information that is trying to emerge from the field around you. In other words, the field between you and the client may be "knocking you out," so to speak, in order for you to gain greater detachment and discover new insights and information otherwise outside of your ordinary mindset. If you feel free enough to follow this noncognitive path, it will then make it easier to recall your learned skills.[93]

In practice, there is a natural rhythm between your cognitive and noncognitive mindsets, while working. Sometimes, you feel quite clear and linear and at other times, your mind might become cloudy, unfocused, or fatigued. If you are able to follow the flow between both and appreciate each, it can be very helpful; not only to you, but also to those with whom you work.

This point reminds me of a television interview that Arny and I did, some years ago. I was a bit uptight and wasn't able to think logically and clearly. In other words, I was having a noncognitive moment, in which I was knocked out of my ordinary awareness and unable to speak clearly about the questions posed by the interviewer. Fortunately, I was able to let go and spacetime dream a bit, without anyone knowing it! By dropping out of the interview momentarily and letting the field guide me, I suddenly remembered something deep and important that I longed to say to the public, but had forgotten about. Once I spoke about what was in my heart, I felt myself naturally returning to my logical train of thought.

Common Ground between You and Your Client(s) and the Fullness of "Empty" Space

There is one more benefit of spacetime dreaming that I feel is very important for your work. It connects to the idea of nonlocality that I mentioned in earlier chapters. In his book, *Dance of the Ancient One*,[94] Arny speaks of a magical experience that often occurs when you experience *spacetime curvature*. In those moments, you frequently connect with a *common ground* or *shared field* between you and those with whom you are working. That is, insights you gain in this state often connect magically and deeply with the person or people with whom you are working.

Pre-Exercise Warm-Up

Before exploring the main exercise in this chapter, it's important to try the following warm-up exercise (which is adapted from the many exercises in Arny's book, *Dance of the Ancient One)* to gain an experience of spacetime dreaming, in a general way. Then, in the main exercise, you'll explore how your spacetime dreaming experiences carry special qualities of your deep facilitator substyle. You'll need paper, something to write with, and some markers, if you have them.

Please use as much space as you need for your spacetime dreaming experience; just be sure to be careful and respect your own body limitations. When you are actually with your clients, groups, or organizations, you might do this exercise in such a subtle way that no one else sees what you are doing. In those moments, even the most subtle motions of being moved by the universe can bring powerful and important information.

1. Think of a question that is on your mind and write it down.

2. Now, stand if you can (or do this in your chair). Take a moment to relax and breathe deeply. Relax a bit more and try to drop out of your ordinary mindset, temporarily. As you breathe and let go, begin to

notice the earth beneath your feet, and sense how the spot you are on is part of the larger earth, and also part of the larger universe.

3. Now, feel the universe's spaces all around you and imagine letting the universe begin to curve you and move you about. That is, let yourself be moved (carefully), like a leaf on the breeze, as you begin to move and dance. Continue to breathe and feel yourself *being moved,* and *even let the universe move you a bit unpredictably* (please take care of your body and physical limitations). As you move, trust and notice tiny experiences, images, or feelings that arise inside of you.

4. Finally, ask yourself what that experience brought you, just now. What might it be telling you? And what does it tell you about the question you asked? Make a note about the answers to these questions and also, sketch a little drawing to capture that experience.

About the Main Exercise

Now, I'd like to give you an exercise to experience the universe moving you *while working with someone.* You can do this alone, imagining that you are working with someone, or you can do it with a partner, where one person is the facilitator and one the client. If you are together with three people, one of you can be the facilitator, one the client, and the other can be the helper who leads the facilitator through the exercise and encourages the facilitator to follow her or his dreaming process. Once again, the focus is mainly on the therapist/facilitator, with the permission of the client. I will write the exercise as if you are a therapist working with a partner who is the client. Once again, adapt it to your own particular situation.

The exercise is noncognitive, so I cannot perfectly explain it in a linear fashion! Please use the steps of the exercise as a general guide and adapt them to your experience and situation.

First, as the facilitator, you will talk about the sensory-grounded channels that you normally use in your work. Then, you'll begin to work with your client. As you do that, you'll notice a moment when you become *noncognitive*. That is, you begin to feel fatigued, spacey, unknowing, distracted, or some other nonlinear experience. And even if this does not happen, for the sake of practice, please stop after five minutes and let yourself begin to experiment with spacetime dreaming.

With the client's permission, you'll take some time to let go and feel the field, as it curves and moves you about. Please do literally get up, if you can, and move, as you just did in the previous exercise. You'll continue moving until your motions become a little bit unpredictable. This is very important. Most of us tend to organize our movements to appear in a certain way. But if you are able to let go a bit more and let the spaces around you move you, you will discover how unpredictable movements can arise. As you do that, you'll watch for new insights and experiences to emerge. Use your awareness to catch quick experiences that arise, and unfold them with any channels you like, such as adding sound, more movement, perhaps drawing, singing, visions, body postures, etc. Most importantly, you'll sense how your experiences influence and form your deep facilitator substyle.

When you begin to work with the client again (or imagine working with her or him), bring the new information or experiences that arose while spacetime dreaming into your interaction in some way and let it influence your style. For example, perhaps as you are moving, you spontaneously imagine a dream figure in the atmosphere between you and the client. You can experiment bringing this figure into your work with the other person, by talking about it, acting it out, etc. Or perhaps your spacetime dreaming experience will bring you a new insight about your work that you did not have before. Bring this into your work with your client, in any way that feels natural for you.

The Therapist's Spacetime Dreaming Mind and Style Exercise

1. Therapist: Discuss/act out your ordinary primary substyle of working with others. What sensory-grounded channels do you think you use most? Make a note.

2. Now, begin to work with your client. In the first five minutes, You should notice if/when a noncognitive moment arises. That is, perhaps you feel spacey, unknowing, tired, can't think, uncertain, or blank. Please stop, there. Even if you don't notice a noncognitive moment, please stop after five minutes, in order to gain more information. Ask the client for permission to explore spacetime dreaming.

3. If you can, stand up and feel the earth beneath your feet. Take a moment to relax; notice your breathing. Relax a bit more; sense the universe/field all around you, and let it begin to curve and move you about (as if you were floating on the wind like a leaf). Continue being moved about and wait until your movement becomes a little unpredictable (be careful of your body and its limitations). Stay

close to the unpredictable movements of spacetime dreaming. Then, at some point, speak out loud about your experiences. You don't have to know, cognitively, what you are doing just now . . . Just trust your experience, as much as you can.

As you continue to move, notice any slight fantasies, visions, intuitions, movements, etc. that catch your attention. Begin to express and unfold these experiences, in any way that feels natural—for example, through movement sound/singing, poetry, spontaneous drawing, visions, acting out figures, etc. Then, sense how your experience would like to influence your facilitator style. What qualities does it bring? Imagine how you would feel, move, and act as a facilitator, using this aspect of your deep substyle.

4. Wait until your experiences seem to naturally *dream themselves into reality*. That is, until you notice that you begin to naturally relate back to the client. Let your spacetime dreaming experience influence your style and bring in any insights you had, as you continue to work with your client for a few more minutes.

5. Afterwards, chat about what you learned.

    •   Therapist: What was it like for you, as the therapist, to go into your spacetime dreaming experience? What insights did you gain and how did it influence your style? Did it give you access to more information than you had with your cognitive mind? Did your experiences connect in some way with your client's process/experiences? What was it like, to use aspects of your deep substyle with your client?

- Client: Please give feedback to the therapist about *your experience* of what happened.

- Therapist: Imagine how you might bring spacetime dreaming into your actual work with people, especially when you are fatigued, confused, or feeling spacey.

- Therapist: Make notes or a song, poem, or drawing about your experiences and learning.

Experiences from Class Participants

When I asked some of my class participants about their experiences with this exercise, most of them said it was a great relief to let go, at some point, and not feel so attentive and anxious about getting it all "right."

One woman said that it was fun and creative. She felt she could relax and was not so frozen in her position.

A man realized that he often has language difficulties while working with people, because he works in English, which is not his first language. When he let himself go into spacetime dreaming, he realized that it is not only a language problem he suffers from, but rather, a part of him is asking him to drop out and gain information in other ways.

Another person said she tends to listen a lot to her clients and is very quiet and subtle about her interventions. To her great surprise, when she went into spacetime dreaming, she began to talk a lot! She felt like a tube, in which she would allow herself to speak, as if she were a channel for new information.

Others had a visceral sense of how going into spacetime dreaming connected deeply with their client's process.

Finding a Thread between Your Deep Substyle Experiences

As you come to the end of this part of the book, you have had a number of experiences of various aspects and qualities of your deep substyle. Now, I'd like to help you see if there is a connection between your various deep substyle experiences. So, take a moment to recall and make a note about the following:

- The ten-minute break experience you had in the beginning of the book (Chapter 3)

- The addition of your primary and secondary substyles (Chapter 16)

- The unique child style that you found in Chapter 17

- The qualities that you found in a person who has been special to you, in your life (Chapter 18)

- The experience and qualities that arose out of a special earth spot (Chapter 19)

- The feelings and qualities that you discovered in this chapter, when you experienced spacetime dreaming.

Look over all of these experiences. Gaze at what you wrote down and intuitively sense if there is a connecting thread, or threads, linking all of them. The words or images may be somewhat different, but perhaps you will sense common elements that run throughout these experiences. When you sense elements that flow throughout your experiences, capture them with a few words. Write them down.

Finally, take a moment to sense how these qualities and your deep substyle have always been in the background, influencing what you do in life and in your work, but you may not have been consciously aware of them.

When you are ready, turn to the last part of the book, where we'll begin to see how all of your substyles are part of a larger mythic dance that moves you as a facilitator.

Embracing the Many Facets of Your Nature

A Short Vignette

I N THE LAST two parts of the book, you learned about, and experimented with, the various substyles of your work. Each substyle reveals an important facet of your unique way of facilitating. Together, they form the beauty and uniqueness of your facilitator style. I'll go much more into this process, in the last section of the book.

Take a moment now to remember some of the learning you gained about your rainbow of styles. Perhaps some of this learning will connect to experiences you had exploring your "gifts of imperfection" in Part Two.

Before going further, I want to share with you something that popped up spontaneously one day while I was editing this book. I felt a bit stuck and decided to let my spacetime dreaming experiences guide me as to how to go further. As I felt the universe moving me, a video that I had seen some months ago popped into my head.

It took me a bit of time to realize why this video was emerging in the moment. Then, it dawned on me that the events in that video emphasized, for me, the importance of valuing *all facets of ourselves and our full processes, not only as facilitators, but in life as a whole*, including the beautiful and the fallible, as well as the deepest spirit that moves us. It also exemplified how embracing the many aspects of our natures can positively affect and contribute to our world. I am aware that this goes a bit outside of the scope of the book, but I hope that my spacetime dreaming experience is meaningful to you.

The video had to do with the 2016 awards ceremony for the Nobel Prize for Literature. The prize was being given to Bob Dylan. Dylan himself was not present, but Patti Smith, the singer/songwriter, punk rocker, poet, and visual artist was there, to accept the award on Dylan's behalf.

The ceremony and atmosphere had a regal quality. Everyone on the stage was dressed in light and dark formal attire. Before Smith appeared, the Nobel Award for Medicine was presented and a beautiful rendition of the classical piece "Serenade," by Jean Sibelius, was played, by the Royal Stockholm Philharmonic Orchestra. Afterwards, the Swedish commentator let the audience know that soon they would hear a very different kind of music.[95]

After receiving the Nobel Award for Literature on behalf of Dylan, Smith, accompanied by the Philharmonic, began to sing Dylan's song, "A Hard Rain's a Gonna Fall."[96] She sang the first verse. Then, upon approaching the second verse of the song, she became quite choked up and was not able to go on. She hesitated many times, but could not continue singing.

After some time, Smith looked up and said, shyly, to the audience, "I'm sorry, I'm so nervous." She repeated this thought once again. She paused and waited for some time until she was able to regain her inner composure. She then signaled to the orchestra that she was ready to begin. She completed the song in what was to me a very beautiful and poignant way, as she sang Dylan's words about the injustice, suffering, and despair in our world: "... *I heard ten-thousand whisperin' and nobody listenin'.*"[97]

I was so moved by hearing her sing Dylan's words about the state of our world, and at the same time, to witness her struggle to sing and her ability, albeit very shyly, to speak so honestly about her nervousness, in such a public and formal setting. I had tears in my eyes as I watched, and so did many in the crowd. *The New Yorker* magazine described Smith as transcendent and recounted the scene in this way:

> "Listening to Smith sing his song—and watching as audience members, dressed in their finest, wiped their eyes, blindly reached for each other, seemed unable to exhale."

For me, Smith was showing in such an honest way what it means to open up to our full selves and process. It is not fair to think of all of this in technical terms, but I can't help pondering that her primary intention was to sing Dylan's song. Yet, she faltered, as a secondary experience of nervousness, which was not intended, emerged. She had the courage to speak about those feelings and was then, finally, able to sing the last verses. At that moment, as the notes and words flowed out of her, I felt as though her deep essence, and the essence of the song, transcended any barriers between herself and the audience. The music and her genuine presence seemed to reach everyone.

After watching this, it became even more apparent to me how important it is to flow with all the parts of ourselves in our work and in our lives. Many of us hope to be perfect and polished and to manifest our most preferred and sparkling style in all we do! And that is a noble(!) intention! Yet, it is our *total* process, with its human, fallible, vulnerable, awesome, and beautiful elements, that makes us who we are and that creates our unique way of working. This in turn, transcends boundaries and connects most deeply, not only with those we work with, but with the larger world.

Now, let's turn to the last section, where you will also have a chance to embrace and flow with the many colors and qualities of your facilitator style and to experience it as a mythic dance that is deep within you, that can enrich both your work and your life as a whole.

PART V

Your Process Oriented Style and Dance

*I*N THIS LAST *section of the book, I'd like to begin to pull some of your learning together and explore how your substyles are part of what I call your facilitator's mythic "dance."*

CHAPTER 21

The Animated Facilitator

*Great dancers are not great because of their technique,
they are great because of their passion.*[98]

—Martha Graham, U.S. dancer and choreographer

T HROUGHOUT THE BOOK, you have had the opportunity to explore the dimensions and qualities of your rainbow of substyles, each of which is a crucial aspect of your facilitator art. Now, in this final section of the book, let's take a wider view and explore the way in which your substyles are part of a larger facilitator *dance* that moves you while working. This dance is not a fixed or static state. Rather it is a *process* or *flow* between *all of your substyles*.

When you are in touch with its overall flow, the dance is like an effortless art that moves you. To feel most at home while working, you need to be in touch with this flow, as it winds and curves between the various substyles of your work.

You'll also learn, in the next chapter, that your facilitator dance grows out of a *basic* and *mythic dream pattern* that has been guiding you throughout your life.

Substyles and the Animated Facilitator

As an artist and puppet maker, I can't help but imagine facilitators and their dance in terms of puppets or marionettes! Imagine that you are the marionette in the picture below. You have various strings, each of which represents one of your substyles.

At a given moment, while you are working, you will sense that one of your (substyle) strings is pulled or tugged upon and begins to move you. At another moment, you will notice a different string being drawn on, as another substyle wants to emerge. When you follow the various motions, your substyles come to life in your work. As time passes, one string and then another begins to move you, and eventually you find yourself in the *flow* of your larger facilitator dance!

Most of us are not conscious of our strings being pulled while working. We tend to focus on one substyle and don't realize, or *want* to realize, when another string (or substyle) is beginning to move. Why? Many facilitators would like to remain only in their primary style. Others would like to be connected to their deep style all the time. This is totally natural! However, it does not embrace the fullness and beauty of your multidimensional nature and process.

A deeply democratic attitude would generously embrace *all of your substyles* as central to your unique way of working. Your primary substyle is crucial, just as your secondary, momentary, and deep substyles bring deeper dreaming experiences and qualities to your work. Sometimes, one or two substyles might emerge as you are working, and at other times, three or four. A process-oriented approach to your style focuses on the *awareness* of which substyle is trying to emerge in a given moment, how it wants to influence your work, and ultimately, the beauty of your whole facilitator dance; a flow that is more than the sum of its individual parts.

So, what happens if you do not follow the way you are being moved or animated in a given moment? Although this resistance to the pull is natural, you will tend to become incongruent, inadvertently convey double signals, become bored, tired, burned out, etc. In other words, your dance becomes a little awkward! Also, if you do not notice when one substyle or another wants to emerge, it will potentially disrupt your learning or ability to recall your skills, until it is noticed, as I discussed in Part II of the book. Greater awareness of your dance of substyles makes your work more fluid and creative, and less effortful. Your work will come to life in your own inimitable way.

Where Do the Strings Come from and Who Is the Great Puppeteer?

In the next chapter, you'll learn that your special substyles (or strings) are not at all random, but rather arise from a *basic mythic pattern* that has been guiding you throughout life. You

will see that the energies and qualities of your substyles can be found in these early dream patterns.

Let me illustrate it, in this way. Imagine that in the picture on the right, the little marionette figure represents you, and the attached strings are connected to your various substyles. If I could reproduce this picture in color, you would see that each substyle is represented by a separate color in order to express your *rainbow* of styles. The "strings" and substyles, as you can see, flow out of a basic mythic pattern.

If I were you, I would wonder, who is the great puppeteer, who is animating and pulling on your strings as you work? Each of you will have your own idea about this. Some call it God. Others might call it the Tao. As I mentioned earlier, Arny calls this great puppeteer our *Processmind*, which, as you remember, is the subtle, creative, and organizing intelligence behind our spontaneous experiences.

Now, let's explore the basic mythic pattern behind your unique style, and finally, in Chapter 23, you'll have the opportunity to practice flowing with your overall facilitator dance in action.

CHAPTER 22

The Mythic Dream Pattern Behind Your Style

Without dreams, the artist would perish.[99]
—Roger Asselin, U.S. artist

*I*N THIS CHAPTER, *you'll see how your overall facilitator dance, with its basic substyle energies, is mythic for you; meaning, fundamental to your nature and part of a guiding pattern that is behind your life and work.*

Many years ago, Carl Jung said that early childhood dreams were predictive of our chosen professions. Years later, Arny took that idea further and discovered that our earliest childhood dreams (as well as first memories in life) not only predict our professions, but are basic organizing patterns that guide us throughout life.[100] These recurring mythic patterns, for example, organize our relationships and even our chronic body symptoms and near-death experiences.[101] We are born with these mythic patterns, and they are always in the background, *dreaming us* on our life paths; though, most often, without our awareness.

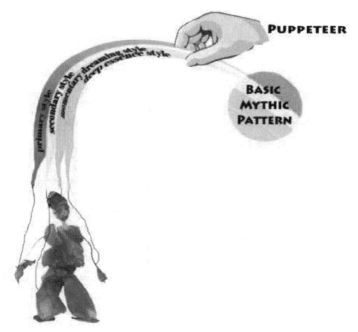

Similarly, I have been fascinated to realize that early memories and dreams *also* contain the energies of your substyles and the overall basic patterns behind your facilitator style! Take a look once again at the picture to the left, where I illustrate the way in which your substyles flow out of your basic mythic pattern. These substyles, in turn, become the "strings" that animate you and bring your work to life. Therefore, the overall dream pattern and the qualities or energies behind your substyles are *mythic* for you; meaning that they accompany and move you, throughout your life and in your work.

Childhood Dream/Memory and Your Substyles

In this chapter, I'd like to give you a chance to explore your mythic pattern, as it appears in your earliest childhood dream or memory, and how the energies of various figures in that dream connect to your substyles. (You could also do this exercise by focusing on the first dream or big experience you had when you began studying your chosen profession. You can find an exercise based specifically on this, in my book, *Alternative to Therapy*.[102])

To begin, let me say a bit more about the nature of dreams and memories. If you look closely at your childhood dream or memory, you'll notice that some parts of the dream are *closer to your awareness* and *identity* (more primary), whereas others are *further away* (secondary). Still other parts, or aspects, of your dream or memory are even further away (more tertiary and closer to the Essence Level). Upon further examination of the dream parts and their energy qualities, you will notice that they correlate with your facilitator substyles. For example, the energy of a primary figure in the dream will connect to your primary substyle, etc.

An Example

Let me first give you an example from my own childhood dream. As a young child, I had a dream that recurred many times. (Many childhood dreams recur.) In the dream, I am in the basement of my father's furniture warehouse at night. I am running away from three guys with guns who are chasing me. I get to an elevator. Depending on the evening, the dream would alternate between three different endings. Sometimes the elevator opened and I got in, went up, and was safe. On other nights, the men would get in the elevator with me and go up, too! In the third ending, the elevator didn't come at all. That was a bad night!

Now, I'll connect the parts of my dream with my substyles. The figure in the dream that is closest to my identity is the little girl, who has a basically playful and good-hearted nature and energy. This correlates with the quality and energy of my *primary* substyle as a facilitator, which is quite related and warmhearted, and often playful.

A more secondary figure and energy in the dream is conveyed by the men coming after me with their direct and strong energy. This type of powerful energy is further from my identity and is connected to my *secondary* facilitator substyle. If I don't use this powerful energy consciously, it might pop up unconsciously; for example, in the form of an inner critic or a body symptom, as I am working.

The tertiary or deep essence figure in the dream is the elevator. For me, the energy and feeling of the elevator as it goes up is spiritual, detached, and full of dreaming and creativity. This is a part of me that is even further from my awareness, yet is central to my basic nature. This energy and quality is connected to my *deep* substyle and way of working as a facilitator. see the diagram on the next page, where I illustrate the connection between dream figures and my substyles.

Sometimes, the sequence with which your substyles emerge while you are working will follow the exact pattern that they appear in your dream/memory. For example, I will often, at first, feel close to my primary substyle of being warmhearted and related with my clients. Then, there will be moments when I want to be more direct and linear (secondary substyle). If I do not notice this secondary substyle arising, I might begin to feel a bit nervous or unsure of the direction I am taking with my client (due to feeling chased, so to speak, by this critical and more direct, powerful part of me). Finally, there are frequently moments when I become spacey or tired (the elevator), which, if followed, would bring a sense of detachment, dreaming, and greater creativity.

While this progression will often be present while I work, my substyles can also appear in an *unpredictable* sequence. As Arny says in his new book, *The Leader's Second Training*, we can know the various parts in your childhood dream, but exactly *how* they will appear in a given moment is utterly unpredictable.[103]

However, no matter when and how your special qualities emerge while you are working, the dance is still utterly *you*. Who you are is irrepressible. Just as we might see a number of different types of Picasso's paintings and know that he painted them all,[104] your style shines across all the variations and alleyways through which it expresses itself.

About the Exercise

Now, I'd like to give you a chance to think about your earliest dream or memory and how it relates to your substyles. Let me tell you a little about the exercise.

First, you will recall your primary, secondary, and deep styles. I will not include your momentary dreaming substyle, because it arises so spontaneously that it is not characteristic of you over time. To remember your substyles, recall any of the experiences you had in this book until now, and take time to especially feel their energy qualities.

Then, you'll tell your earliest childhood dream, or the first memory you remember in your life, and identify three of its central aspects. These aspects could be, for example, people, animals, objects, or experiences, such as flying or dancing. Of course, your dream or memory may not appear to have three different elements! If your dream (or memory) seems to have only one or two aspects, look again and notice other aspects that you might not have noticed or thought of before, such as the atmosphere of the overall dream, or the feeling of a particular room. You might also identify a figure or aspect of the dream that is *implied,* but not quite seen directly, such as hearing the footsteps of an approaching figure, but you do not see the figure, yet.

Then, you'll make associations to those dream aspects. That means: notice what feelings or experiences pop up, when you think about each of them. You'll then sense and express the *energy qualities* of each of those dream figures or parts.

After that, I'd like you to *intuitively* connect these figures/ parts and their energies to the energies of your facilitator substyles. Please stay close to the *energies* of each figure, because this will help you connect with it, most completely. I will not stress the *intellectual* understanding of the dream. Rather, I would like you to let the connections between dream parts/ energies and your substyles pop up, intuitively. When I have done this in my classes, participants were quite surprised at the connections between their substyle energies and the energies found in aspects of their dreams. This helped them sense how there is a guiding mythic pattern and special energies that move with them in life and inform all they do.

If you have trouble finding a connection between the energy of one of your substyles and one of the aspects of your dream that you chose, take another look at the dream/memory. See if there is *another part* of the dream that has the same type of energy as that substyle. Remember to notice such things as the dream's overall atmosphere, or the feeling quality of a particular location or figure.

Finally, you'll have time to reflect on your experience and sense the larger pattern of the dream or memory that is moving you as a facilitator. You can do the exercise as innerwork, or together with a partner who interviews you.

You'll need paper and pen, for notes.

Exploring the Basic Pattern Behind Your Facilitator Style

1. Take a moment to recall and make a note about your various substyles. You can look back at notes from the earlier exercises in the book, or just think about your substyles, now.

   - What is your ordinary *primary substyle* like? That is, the substyle that is closest to your awareness and identity. Describe some of its qualities and act it out with your hands, face, and posture. Notice the *energy* quality of that substyle and make a note about it.

- What is your *secondary substyle* like? That is, the substyle that is further from your awareness, and about which you are a bit shy. Describe some of its qualities and act it out with your hands, face, and posture. Sense the *energy* quality of that substyle and make a note about it.

- Describe some of the qualities of your *deep substyle*, which is even further from your awareness. Recall any of the experiences you have had, in the last section of the book. Or go back to the exercise in Chapter 3, where you imagined having ten minutes free in the day, in which you could do anything you wanted to do that drew you to it. If you don't remember that experience, try it briefly, now. Feel the quality and *energy* of that deep essence experience and make a note about it.

2. Now, tell a childhood dream, or earliest memory. Identify and make associations to three central or main aspects of that dream/memory. To make an association, simply ask yourself: "What do I associate with, or what quickly comes to mind, when I think about this or that aspect?" Then, one after the other, *act out* those three aspects; exaggerate them, and especially sense their *basic energy qualities*. Once you can feel these energies, make a quick sketch of them on your paper and give each one a name.

3. Now, take time to intuitively connect these dream/memory energies to the energies of your primary, secondary, and deep substyles. Write these connections down. (If you have trouble connecting one of

your substyle energies to a dream part, look once again at the dream. See if there is *another part* of the dream that you had not previously noticed, that has the same type of energy as that substyle. For example, you might notice the dream's overall atmosphere or the energy quality of a particular location or figure.)

- Intuitively consider the larger mythic pattern from your childhood dream/memory that is moving you and trying to come into your awareness through your substyles as a facilitator.

- In what way are your substyles and their energies *mythic* for you? That is, how do they appear, not only in your early dream/memory, but also throughout your life?

Arny's Childhood Dream and Style

Here is another example, this time of Arny's childhood dream, which might give you more insight into the connection between a childhood dream and substyles. In his dream, Arny, as a little boy, was washing his father's car. A bear comes and continually chases him, through the car and then, out and into ever greater circles.

Arny's primary substyle is like his father, kind and scientific. His secondary substyle is like the bear, with its spontaneous nature and powerful energy. His deep substyle is like the ever-increasing circles. If you know Arny, you would realize that this circling is behind his movement from physics to psychology, and his drive to expand Process Work into ever larger circles. What began with individual work, then grew to relationship work, group work, many other areas, and finally, to embracing and understanding our relationship to the earth and universe. In practice, he moves between his warmhearted father and scientific nature, spontaneous energies that come through him, and finally, to dropping out and letting the universe move and inform him, as he is working.

I hope this experience shows you that your overall facilitator dance and its substyles are patterned in your earliest childhood dream or memory. This mythic pattern is behind and moving you as you work, though you are probably not aware of it. With greater awareness, your unique myth and style can be used even more consciously to enrich your work, bring your most unique gifts to those you work with, and help you to feel more at home and fluid, in all that you do.

Now, turn to the last chapter, in which I will give you the opportunity to flow with this overall pattern and your substyles, as you sense your facilitator dance, in action.

CHAPTER 23

The Artistry and Flow of Your Unique Style

"I had no plans of any destination.
I wish to flow like a river."[105]

—Lailah Gifty Akita,
Ghanaian writer and bio scientist

I N LIFE, WE are constantly evolving, changing, growing, and being moved by a flow of experiences. In the same way, facilitators are continually *in process*. In other words, your overall facilitator style is not a static *thing*, but rather a *flowing process* that moves you, as you work.

As we saw in the last chapter, your facilitator substyles are patterned in your earliest childhood dream or memory. That is, they appear in the figures and parts of your childhood dream or memory pattern. They are not random, but embedded in the mythic guiding pattern that moves you. Therefore, your substyles and their energies are central to your basic nature; they are mythic energies that accompany you throughout life. As a facilitator, teacher, therapist, coach, or other helper, they inform your work and are the gifts and powers that animate all that you do.

In this final chapter, you'll have a chance to bring together much of what you have been learning in this book. You will be able to experience your facilitator dance by becoming aware of, and joining with, each substyle as it arises while working. With time and practice, you will no longer mechanically focus on the individual substyles, but rather, will find yourself flowing in the stream of your unique dance. You will begin to appreciate how you are moved by the mythic pattern that has always been in the background of your work, and how the energies of your substyles bring your skills to life, in your own inimitable way.

As I personally become aware of, and flow with, my full artist's palette of substyles, I notice an increasing sense of satisfaction in my work. Rather than remaining solely with one of my substyles, I am more able to flow with any one of my substyles as it begins to emerge, and allow it to influence and enhance my work. In addition, I have the opportunity to *consciously* draw upon any of the substyles in my artist's palette, in order to amplify and widen the work I am doing in a given moment.

I recall one session I had with a client. In the beginning, I was using my primary substyle, which was quite related and attentive. After a while, I noticed that I had an inner critic (an indication of my secondary substyle emerging) that was making me a bit doubtful about the direction in which our work was going. I told my client about my self-doubt, and she said that, actually, she had a critic that was bothering her, too! After some time exploring that (shared) critic together, I noticed that I became a bit tired and unfocused and realized that my deep substyle was trying to emerge. I asked my client's permission to explore this feeling. As I let go and let myself dream, I had an inner vision of how my client might deal with her problems and her critic. I told her about my vision and this was quite helpful to her.

Experiencing the Flow of Your Facilitator Dance

In this final awareness exercise, you will have the chance to experience the flow of your own facilitator dance. The beauty of this practice lies within its simplicity. Basically, you will notice and try to consciously use and flow with each substyle as it emerges, allowing it to influence your work in whatever way feels best for you and your client. This practice has been a very helpful and energizing experience for my students, and I hope will be for you, as well.

In the beginning of the exercise, I will ask you to recall your various substyles and their energies and write these down on a piece of paper. You can always go back to this paper, to remind yourself of the substyles that may be emerging as you work. In addition, you can also consciously draw upon any one of your substyles if you feel stuck and do not know how to go forward.

I suggest that you begin working with your primary substyle. Use it consciously, even exaggerate it a bit more, and then, as you continue to work, use your awareness to notice when any of your other substyles are trying to emerge. There are some clues that will help you to notice when one substyle or another is arising. For example, you might notice your secondary substyle trying to emerge through one of your double signals. If so, and if the situation allows, amplify that double signal slightly, to discover what it is trying to express and how it would like to influence your way of working in the moment.

You might also notice your momentary dreaming substyle emerging. That is, you may notice a slight "flirt" that grabs your attention. Depending on the situation, use your creativity to unfold that flirt and see what new information it is trying to bring to your style and to the client's situation. Or, you may notice a slight movement tendency happening in your body. Follow it, let it unfold a bit, and notice what it is expressing. Then, sense how this experience wants to influence your style in the moment.

At another point, you may notice that your deep substyle is trying to emerge when, for example, you feel tired, blank, unknowing, or like you have gotten to the limits of what you know. Or you might notice any of the other experiences that you explored in Part IV trying to emerge. In those moments, allow your deep substyle to emerge and influence the way you are working. You might, for example, let go of your ordinary mind and let the universe move you about, in order to discover new information. At any moment, your primary substyle (or any other substyle) might return; please follow it and let it influence your work once more.

For purposes of practice, I would suggest that you state out loud which substyle is emerging. By doing this, you will be able to consciously manifest the gifts of that substyle, and then be free to let go of it and flow with any other substyle that arises. Remember, if you don't notice a substyle emerging, that substyle might hold on so tightly, that it makes it difficult to flow with any others!

As you work, one substyle might arise, or several. As I said earlier, ultimately, when you are in the flow of your style, you will no longer need to focus on each individual substyle. Rather, you'll be in touch with the greater dance that moves you.

Once again, the focus is on your awareness and learning. You can do the exercise alone, imagining that you are working with a client, student, couple, or organization. Or, you can do the exercise with a partner.

Flowing with Your Substyles and Facilitator Dance

1. To begin, take some time to recall some of the qualities/energies of your primary, secondary, and deep substyles. Make a note on your paper about these substyles and their energies, so you can refer back to them, if needed. Also remember that your momentary deep style emerges in those moments when a tiny flirt catches your attention, or when you notice a subtle movement tendency happening in your body.

2. Begin to work with your partner (or do this alone, imagining that you are working with a client, organization, couple, etc.) using your primary substyle. Bring this substyle out consciously, in some way. Then, as you continue to work, notice when any of your other substyles begin to emerge. When one arises, feel it, sense how it would like to influence your style in the moment, and let it influence your work. Continue to work with your client and notice if/when another style emerges, and do the same, etc.

   If, at any time, you feel stuck or unable to notice what is happening, look at your list of substyles and sense or choose one that might enrich the work you are doing in that moment. At some point, you may notice that you no longer concentrate on each individual substyle, but find yourself in the stream of your larger facilitator "dance."

3. Finally, ponder the following:

- What was it like to notice and bring in your substyles consciously, as they arose?

- How did this affect your work?

- What did you learn about yourself and your overall facilitator style?

- How did the use of your substyles influence the way you used any practical skills that you have learned?

- Did you get to the point where you were flowing in the stream of your larger facilitator dance?

For your information, another way to do this exercise is to first get in contact with your Essence Level experience of spacetime dreaming. Once you let go and feel moved, it may be even easier to notice and open up to the various substyles that emerge.

Fluid Awareness and Artistry

As you flow and swing between substyles, you become more fluid as a facilitator. As your innate gifts blend fluidly with the skills you have learned, you begin to identify with the mythic dance that moves you. In that moment, the true artist behind your work comes fully to life.

CONCLUSION
Your Seamless Dance

A FEW YEARS AGO, I made my first stop-motion animation. Perhaps due to my many years of studying dance
and choreography, and my fascination with this art
form, I was driven to find out if I could get a little 4-inch-tall
cloth and wire figure that I had made to "dance." I was a total
novice, but I was compelled to try.

I set my little figure up on a makeshift stage, placed her in a pose, and took a picture. I then moved her ever so slightly and took another photo. I repeated this sequence for what seemed like a million times! I had read about this process, but I had no idea how painstaking it would be. I hunched over and concentrated so intensely that I ended up with quite a backache. I wondered if all that effort was necessary, or would even work!

Then, something amazing happened. When I finally played back the video, it took my breath away. Each individual pose gave way, as my originally *inanimate* figure began to dance, all by herself! She suddenly seemed to have a life and spirit of her own. It blew my mind![106]

In the same way, throughout this book, I have taken you slowly, piece by piece, through the various "steps" and "gestures" of your facilitator style. In the early parts of the book, I spoke about your style with broad strokes, exploring how your most unusual, different, even weird, nature holds the keys to your special way of working. As you explored learning difficulties and "cracks" in your facilitator pot, paradoxically, these became doorways into the special qualities that make your work individual, creative, and effective.

I stressed that each of us is unique, like the vast diversity of nature, and that this uniqueness is the source and gift of your facilitator style. Your special nature enlivens and brings your skills to life most usefully and effectively. It is this part of you that most often draws people to you. However, you are frequently not aware of your gifts; that is why I called it your *secret power*.

In the middle of the book, you began to see that your style is multidimensional; it contains a rainbow of individual substyles. With a deeply democratic attitude, you embraced and explored each substyle and practiced using each in action.

You discovered that you have the gift of a wide palette of colors or substyles that you can call on and notice while working.

The last part of the book focused on bringing everything together. Here, you discovered that the different qualities and energies of your substyles are not random. Rather, they have always been basic to your nature and can be found patterned in your early dreams and memories. You had the opportunity to experience the larger flow or process between all of your substyles as they emerged while working. Rather than remaining stuck in any one substyle, you experienced it as a grand dance, from one "step" to another. When these work in tandem with each other, this dance reveals the richness and beauty of your unique way of working.

Hopefully, experiencing this flow gave you a sense of how your style is not *fixed*, but rather, a continually evolving *process* or *dance*. This dance is more than the sum of its parts. When you are in it, it can't be defined exactly, yet it is the living power and spirit that moves you in life, and in your work. Like the goddess Kannon that I mentioned in the Preface, your style is like a guiding spirit that is beneath the water, a constant, flowing power influencing you and bringing your special way of working to life.

So, while your style is something to learn about and grow into, as I have said previously, it is also something to *remember*. When you are in touch with it, it can bring a great sense of ease and wellness, as it uses your skills in a most effective and effortless way. If you lose track of your skills, if you become exhausted, unsure or burned out, your facilitator dance is always there to guide you.

Like my stop-motion endeavor, when you begin to learn about your style, it takes time, as you become increasingly aware of and experience your substyles in action—that is, exploring one "step," so to speak, after another. Yet, ultimately, individual steps give way to the larger seamless dance that moves you.

While many of us would like to be close to our unique styles *all the time*, it would not be natural. As Arny says, each of us cycles through natural *phases*.[107] With a generous and deeply democratic heart, you can embrace moments when you tend to favor one style over another, those moments when you are not able to quite swing from one to the next, as well as those exquisite moments when all the individual steps fall away and you are simply living in the stream of your facilitator dance.

I hope this book has shown you that who you are is unique and irreplaceable. You were born with a rich facilitator palette of colors and substyles. This palette brings all you do to life, in your own inimitable way. Remember these gifts and let them live through you. As you model embracing your own unique nature, you simultaneously encourage those individuals, couples, or groups that you work with to embrace and realize their full natures, as well. In this way, your unique facilitator style is the greatest gift you have, for yourself, for those you work with, and for our world.

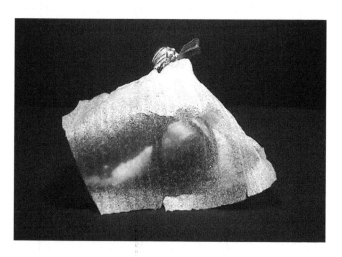

Bibliography

Bailie, Gil. *Violence Unveiled: Humanity at the Crossroads.* New York: Crossroad Publishing, 1995.

Castaneda, Carlos.

A Separate Reality. New York: Touchstone, 1972.

Journey to Ixtlan. New York: Washington Square Press, 1991.

Deshimaru, Taisen. *The Zen Way to Martial Arts: A Japanese Master Reveals the Secrets of the Samurai.* New York, NY: Penguin Books, 1992.

Diamond, Julie, and Sparks, Caroline. *A Path Made by Walking: Process Work in Practice* (2nd Ed.). Santa Fe: Belly Song Press, 2018.

Greene, Robert. *Mastery.* New York: 2012, Penguin Group, 2012.

Hauser, Reini. http://www.reinihauser.net/files/1994.pdf.

Henri, Robert. *The Art Spirit.* New York: Harper & Row, 1984.

Inayat Khan, Hazrat. *The Mysticism of Sound and Music: The Sufi Teaching of Hazrat Inayat Khan.* Boston & London: Shambhala, 1996.

Loori, John Daido. *The Zen of Creativity: Cultivating Your Artistic Life.* New York: Ballantine Books, 2005.

Mecouch, George. *While Psychiatry Slept: Reawakening the Imagination in Therapy.* Santa Fe: Belly Song Press, 2018.

Mindell, Amy.

Metaskills: The Spiritual Art of Therapy (2nd ed.). Portland, OR: Lao Tse Press, 1995.

The Dreaming Source of Creativity: 30 Creative and Magical Ways to Work on Yourself. Portland, OR: Lao Tse Press, 2005.

Alternative to Therapy: A Creative Lecture Series on Process Work (2nd ed.). Portland, OR: Lao Tse Press, 2006.

"Process Work and the Art of Animation," September, 2007. *https://static1.squarespace.com/static/54a386c7e4b07985e3618194/t/557c5d44e4b0d0b21b858e14/1434213700430/animation.pdf*

"The Evolution and Three Branches of Process Theory" (3rd ed.), August 2016. *https://static1.squarespace.com/static/54a386c7e4b07985e3618194/t/57d63f528419c258722075be/1473658719025/2016+Update+of+The+Evolution+of+Process+Theory+wHyperlinks.pdf* .

The Life of Flowers: 80 Art Creations with Flowers and Plants. San Francisco: Blurb, 2017.

Mindell, Arnold.

The Leader's Second Training for Your Life and Our World. Columbus: OH: Gatekeeper Press, 2019.

Conflict: Phases, Forums, and Solutions: For Our Dreams and Body, Organizations, Governments, and Planet. Portland, OR: CreateSpace Independent Publishing Platform, 2017.

Dance of the Ancient One, Portland, OR: Deep Democracy Exchange, 2012.

Processmind: A User's Guide to the Mind of God. Wheaton, IL: Quest Books, 2010.

Earth-Based Psychology: Path Awareness from the Teachings of Don Juan, Richard Feynman, and Lao Tse. Portland, OR: Lao Tse Press, 2007.

Quantum Mind and Healing: How to Listen and Respond to Your Body's Symptoms. Charlottesville, NC: Hampton Roads, 2004.

"Some History, Theory and Practice Beginning with the Dreambody and Including the Quantum Mind and Healing." http://www.aamindell.net/processwork_frame. htm, 2004.

Dreaming While Awake: Techniques for 24-Hour Lucid Dreaming. Charlottesville, VA: Hampton Roads, 2000.

Quantum Mind: The Edge between Physics and Psychology. Portland, OR: Deep Democracy Exchange, 2012. (Original work published by Lao Tse Press, 2000.)

Sitting in the Fire: Large Group Transformation Using Conflict and Diversity. Portland, OR: Deep Democracy Exchange, 2014. (Original work published by Lao Tse Press, 1995.)

The Shaman's Body: A New Shamanism for Transforming Health, Relationships, and the Community. San Francisco: Harper Collins, 1993.

The Leader as Martial Artist: An Introduction to Deep Democracy. Portland, OR: Deep Democracy Exchange, 2014. (Original work published by Harper Collins, 1992)

Coma: Key to Awakening. Boulder, CO: Shambhala, 1989; and *Coma: The Dreambody Near Death.* Portland, OR: Lao Tse Press, 2009.

Working on Yourself Alone: Inner Dreambody Work. Portland, OR: Lao Tse Press, 2000. (Original work published in 1989 by Viking-Penguin-Arkana)

City Shadows: Psychological Interventions in Psychiatry. London & New York: Viking-Penguin-Arkana, 1988.

The Dreambody in Relationships. Portland, OR: Lao Tse Press, 2000. (Original work published in 1987 by Viking-Penguin-Arkana)

Working with the Dreaming Body. Portland, OR: Lao Tse Press, 2000. (Original work published in 1986 by Viking-Penguin-Arkana)

River's Way: The Process Science of the Dreambody. London & New York: Viking-Penguin-Arkana, 1985.

Dreambody: The Body's Role in Revealing the Self. Portland, OR: Lao Tse Press, 2000. (Original work published in 1982 by Sigo Press and in 1986 by Viking-Penguin-Arkana)

Richardson, John. *A Life of Picasso: The Triumphant Years, 1917–1932*. New York, NY: Knopf, 2007.

Stabler, David, Doogie Horner illustrator. *Kid Artists, True Tales of Childhood from Creative Legends*. Philadelphia: Quirk Books, 2016.

Strachan, Alan. *"The Wisdom of the Dreaming Body: On The Relationship Between Childhood Dreams And Adult Illnesses."* http://alanstrachan.com/Dreaming_Childhood.html.

Suzuki, Daesetz.T. *Zen and Japanese Culture*. Princeton, N.J.: Bollingen Foundation Inc., Princeton University Press, 1959.

Suzuki, Daisetz T., Ed. Christmas Humphreys. *The Awakening of Zen*. Boston and London: Shambhala, 1987.

Ueshiba, Kisshomaru. *The Spirit of Aikido*. New York, NY: Kodansha America, Inc, 1988.

Velali, Ioanna, "'Ways of Being': A Creative/Educational Project Exploring the Relationship between Life Myth and the Therapist's Style." Process Work Institute, Portland, OR, May 2016 (A final project submitted in partial fulfillment of the requirements for the Master's degree in Process Work) http://www.processwork.org/files/Finalprojects/Velali,_I_May_2016.pdf

Vowell, Sarah. *Take the Cannoli: Stories from the New World.* New York: Simon and Schuster, 2001._

Watts, Alan. *The Way of Zen.* New York: Vintage Books, 1999.

Zander, Rosamund Stone and Benjamin. *The Art of Possibility: Transforming Professional and Personal Life,* New York: Penguin, 2002.

Endnotes

1. See my animated Worldwork video series at http://www. aamindell.net/worldwork-animated-film

2. Wikipedia contributors. (2018, August 7). Sensō-ji. In *Wikipedia, The Free Encyclopedia*. Retrieved 00:35, August 22, 2018, from https://en.wikipedia.org/w/index. php?title=Sens%C5%8D-ji&oldid=853827216

3. Arny calls the attempt to adapt to a set of cultural norms, "mainstreaming." See his book, *The Leader's Second Training for Your Life and our World*.

4. Tom Waits, http://www.goodreads.com/quotes/70510-my-kids-are-starting-to-notice-i-m-a-little-different.

5. Ibid.

6. https://www.azquotes.com/quote/489887

7. You can find more of my flower art in my book *The Life of Flowers* San Francisco: Blurb, 2017 (http://www.blurb. com/b/8059709-the-life-of-flowers).

8. http://www.goodreads.com/quotes/tag/style?page= 4&utf8=%E2%9C%93 . This quote reminds me of the informative book on Process Work written by Julie Diamond and Caroline Sparks called *A Path Made by Walking* (Santa Fe: Belly Song Press, 2018).

9. *Processmind: A Users Guide to the Mind of God* (Quest Books: Wheaton, Ill., 2010).

10. http://theconversation.com/how-maya-angelou-made-me-feel-27328.

11. Of course, many are drawn to addictive substances, through I do not focus on them in this chapter. For more about Arny's early ideas about addictions and addictive tendencies and Reini Hauser's research on addictions, see http://www.reinihauser.net/files/1994.pdf.

12. Speaking about the warrior, Don Juan says " . . . every item he chooses is a shield that protects him from the onslaughts of the forces he is striving to use. For that purpose you must have a selected number of things that give you great peace and pleasure . . . The things a warrior selects to make his shields are the items of a path with heart." From Carlos Castaneda, *A Separate Reality,* (New York: Touchstone, 1972) pp. 260-262.

13. https://www.huffingtonpost.com/larry-paros/word-origin-comics-get-mo_b_9244666.html.

14. Robert Henri, *The Art Spirit* (New York: Harper & Row, 1984), p. 78.

15. NPR's "All Things Considered" program called, "*At 75, Chick Corea still has that magic touch*" https://www.npr.org/2016/11/13/501592227/at-75-chick-corea-still-has-that-magic-touch, (11/13/16).

16. https://qz.com/835076/leonard-cohens-anthem-the-story-of-the-line-there-is-a-crack-in-everything-thats-how-the-light-gets-in/. Preceding image of the cracked pot from *Shutterstock.com.*

17. Daisetz Teitaro Suzuki, Ed. Christmas Humphreys. *The Awakening of Zen*, (Boston and London; Shambhala, 1987) 59.

18. Wikipedia contributors. (2018, July 11). Kintsugi. In *Wikipedia, The Free Encyclopedia*. Retrieved 01:38, August 3, 2016, from https://en.wikipedia.org/w/index.php?title=Kintsugi&oldid=849838910

19. The School of Life, "Eastern Philosophy - Kintsugi" *You Tube*. Online video clip, https://www.youtube.com/watch?v=EBUTQkaSSTY (accessed 9 September 2018).

20. Article in the UK Guardian. Oliver Burkeman. (2010, April 24) Wabi Sabi: The Beauty in Imperfection: Retrieved from http://www.theguardian.com/lifeandstyle/2010/apr/24/change-your-life-beauty. Also, Leonard Koren writes about the concept of Wabi-Sabi in Wabi-Sabi For Artists, Designers, Poets & Philosophers. http://www.leonardkoren.com/lkwa.html. He says, " . . . broadly, it's the aesthetic that finds beauty in imperfection and transience: in buildings beaten by wind and rain, in rough-hewn objects that hint at their inevitable decay, in the asymmetrical, chipped, off-kilter pottery used in the Japanese tea ceremony . . . It is a beauty of things imperfect, impermanent, and incomplete."

21. The School of Life, "History of Ideas – Wabi-sabi" *You Tube*. Online video clip, https://www.youtube.com/watch?v=QmHLYhxYVjA (accessed 9 September 2017)

22. The Way of Zen (New York: Vintage Books) 196.

23. http://www.goodreads.com/quotes/558213-learn-the-rules-like-a-pro-so-you-can-break

24. Alternative to Therapy (Portland, OR: Lao Tse Press) 339–340.

25. Suzuki op cit., p. 59. Preceding image from Pixabay.com.

26. *Take the Cannoli: Stories from the New World.* (New York: Simon and Schuster, 2001) 209.

27. Jacques Renee. (2013 September 25) *16 Wildly Successful People Who Overcame Huge Obstacles To Get There* http://www.huffingtonpost.com/2013/09/25/successful-people-obstacles_n_3964459.html. Retrieved August 21, 2018. Jacques says about Einstein, "He always received good marks, but his head was in the clouds, conjuring up abstract questions people couldn't understand."

28. Wikipedia contributors. (2018, July 28). Maud Lewis. In *Wikipedia, The Free Encyclopedia.* Retrieved 02:25, August 22, 2018, from https://en.wikipedia.org/w/index.php?title=Maud_Lewis&oldid=852337794

29. Sugar, Rachel. (2017, August 14) *29 Famous People Who Failed before they Succeeded* https://www.independent.co.uk/news/people/success-29-famous-people-failed-jay-z-oprah-winfrey-steven-spielberg-isaac-newton-charles-darwin-a7892406.html Retrieved June 6, 2018)

30. Rosamund Stone Zander and Benjamin Zander, *The Art of Possibility: Transforming Professional and Personal Life.* (New York: Penguin, 2002) 32.

31. Translated by Coleman Barks with John Moyne. http://www.poetseers.org/spiritual-and-devotional-poets/contemp/rumibarks/4-2/index.html accessed August 21, 2018. Thanks to Julita Lukaszuk for telling me about this beautiful poem.

32. Yachats, Oregon newsletter, date unknown. Also this story from Jack Riemer, February 10, 2001, *"Perlman makes his music the hard way"* in the Houston Chronical http://www. chron.com/life/houston-belief/article/Perlman-makes-his-music-the-hard-way-2009719.php Accessed August 17, 2017.

33. For example, two of his recordings that I really like are from his CD: Itzhak Perlman, *Concertos From My Childhood* (https://www.amazon.com/Concertos-Childhood-2CD-Itzhak-Perlman/dp/B010FULK6M) Violin Concerto in B Minor, Op.35: II. Andante and Schueler Konzert Nr 2 Op. 13: II. Adagio.

34. Wikipedia contributors. (2018, August 18). Frida Kahlo. In *Wikipedia, The Free Encyclopedia*. Retrieved 07:03, August 22, 2018, from https://en.wikipedia.org/w/index. php?title=Frida_Kahlo&oldid=855460604

35. Wikipedia contributors. (2018, August 21). Ludwig van Beethoven. In *Wikipedia, The Free Encyclopedia*. Retrieved 16:24, August 22, 2018, from https://en.wiki pedia.org/w/index.php?title=Ludwig_van_Beetho ven&oldid=855838842. Wikipedia says about Beethoven, "By his late 20s his hearing began to deteriorate, and by the last decade of his life he was almost totally deaf. In 1811, he gave up conducting and performing in public but continued to compose; many of his most admired works come from these last 15 years of his life."

36. Rothman, Lily. (2015 December 17). *Here's What Beethoven Did When He Lost His Hearing*. http://time.com/4152023/ beethoven-birthday/ Rothman says about Beethoven, "He even introduced the world to what remains perhaps his most famous composition—the Ninth Symphony—well

after deafness had overtaken him, an irony that produced one of the most poignant moments of his career.

37. https://onbeing.org/programs/joan-halifax-buoyancy-rather-than-burnout-in-our-lives-oct2017/

38. Thanks to Hanoch Piven for his wonderful creativity, to Elaine Kaplan for telling me about Piven's work, and Ajay Noronha for introducing me to Piven and his creative and artistic world!

39. De Waal, Mandy. (2008 August 1). *Symphony of Possibility.* http://www.brainstormmag.co.za/personality-profile/10890-symphony-of-possibility.

40. President Barack Obama speech, honoring Ozawa at the Kennedy Center Honors 2015. CBS News. (2015 December 23). *Conductor Seiji Ozawa's two loves.* http://www.cbsnews.com/news/kennedy-center-honors-conductor-seiji-ozawa/ .

41. Hazrat Inayat Khan. *The Mysticism of Sound and Music: The Sufi Teaching of Hazrat Inayat Khan* (Boston and London: Shambhala 1996) p.i.

42. https://www.michelangelo-gallery.com/quotes.aspx. Preceding image from Shutterstock.com.

43. Daesetz.T. Suzuki. *Zen and Japanese Culture.* (Princeton, N.J.: Bollingen Foundation Inc., Princeton University Press, 1959) 114.

44. In Chapter 18, I speak about one of my own teachers, Ben Thompson, who impressed me in a similar way. Actually, Ben was an earlier teacher of Arny's, as well!

45. Zander and Zander. *The Art of Possibility*, 26.

46. In my book *Metaskills: The Spiritual Art of Therapy* (Portland, OR: Lao Tse Press, 1995) 167–177, I speak about this progression in terms of the Zen story about a mountain.

47. From the Foreword by George Leonard in Taisen Deshimaru's *The Zen Way to Martial Arts: A Japanese Master Reveals the Secrets of the Samurai* (New York, Penguin Books, 1992).

48. *The Spirit of Aikido* (New York, NY: Kodansha America, Inc, 1988) 89–90.

49. Zander and Zander, *The Art of Possibility*, 103.

50. https://en.wikiquote.org/wiki/Talk:Antoni_Gaud%C3%AD. Photo by Wjh31 (Own work - http://lifeinmegapixels.com) [CC BY 3.0 (http://creativecommons.org/licenses/by/3.0)], via Wikimedia Commons

51. *Art: Fantastic Catalan*, 1952, Jan. 28. Retrieved from URL http://content.time.com/time/magazine/article/0,9171,806302,00.html.

52. I first began writing about, and provided exercises for, some of the facilitator's substyles in my book, *Alternative to Therapy: A Creative Lecture Series on Process Work* (Portland, OR: Lao Tse Press, 2006) 333-345.

53. https://sandra-silberzweig.pixels.com/index.html?tab=about.

54. *The Leader as Martial Artist: An Introduction to Deep Democracy* (San Francisco: Harper, 1992).

55. In my book *Alternative to Therapy*, pp. 336–339, I originally called this substyle your "Deep and Hidden" substyle.

56. For more about the different levels, see Arny's *Dreaming While Awake: Techniques for 24 Hour Lucid Dreaming,* (Charlottesville, VA: Hampton Roads, 2000), pp. 13–23 and throughout that book, and also my article on the "*The Evolution and Three Branches of Process Theory, 3rd Edition*" *https://static1.squarespace.com/static/54a386c7e 4b07985e3618194/t/57d63f528419c258722075be/1473658 719025/2016+Update+of+The+Evolution+of+Process+The ory+wHyperlinks.pdf,* 2016.

57. Clipart image.

58. Clipart image.

59. See my *Alternative to Therapy,* pp. 342–343, for further discussion about your Anti-Style.

60. See Arny's book, *Dreaming While Awake.*

61. Ibid.

62. In order to notice flirts, we need what Arny calls *lucid attention*, which is different than our ordinary consciousness. *Lucidity* refers to the ability to notice subtle tendencies and "pre-signals" that are so fleeting that they are not yet stable signals or double signals. Lucid attention requires that we have a mind that is sufficiently open, empty, and foggy or diffused, to notice and nurture subtle experiences. See his book, *Dreaming While Awake, Techniques for 24-Hour Lucid Dreaming.* (Charlottesville, VA: Hampton Roads, 2000) 17-29.

63. From George Mecouch, *While Psychiatry Slept: Reawakening the Imagination in Therapy,* (Santa Fe: Belly Song Press, 2018), 32.

64. See Arny's *Dreaming While Awake,* 104–108.

65. This reminds me of a metaskill I call "fishing." That is, sitting and waiting until a fish swims by and then catching it, and bringing it up. *Metaskills*, 103–122.

66. *From MIT News*, March/April 2016, 11.

67. See Arny's book, *The Leader's Second Training for Your Life and Our World*.

68. It is interesting to note that some therapists, teachers, facilitators, and coaches are more in touch with these deep states when they are working with others than when they are alone in their daily lives. Many therapists have told me that they sink into their deepest selves while working. The atmosphere and context remind them of this state and anchors the experience in their body. However, when they leave their work, they seem to be further away from it. There are instances, however, when people have the opposite experience. They are closer to their deep selves when alone, but when they are working with others, they feel pulled out of it.

69. https://www.timesledger.com/stories/2011/33/at_ent_news_scileppi_henson_momi_20110811.html. Preceding image from iclipart.com.

70. David Stabler, illustrated by Doogie Horner, *Kid Artists, True Tales of Childhood from Creative Legends* (Philadelphia: Quirk Books, 2016).

71. *Alternative to Therapy*, 348–350.

72. In a recent seminar, called "Why You Were Born," Arny and I spoke about this mythic pattern. For much more on this topic, see his book *The Leader's Second Training for Your Life and Our World. (Columbus: Gatekeeper Press, 2019).*

73. Robert Greene, *Mastery* (New York: 2012, Penguin Group, 2012), 19–29.

74. Ibid., p. 26.

75. Ibid., pp. 30–31.

76. Ibid, p.30.

77. Ibid. p. 31.

78. Gil Bailie tells the story in the first paragraph of the "In Gratitude" section of his book, *Violence Unveiled: Humanity at the Crossroads* (New York: Crossroad Publishing, 1995), xv.

79. https://www.goodreads.com/quotes/5934-i-ve-learned-that-people-will-forget-what-you-said-people

80. *The Shaman's Body* (San Francisco: Harper Collins, 1993).

81. Castaneda wrote many books about Don Juan, including such titles as *Journey to Ixtlan* (Washington Square Press; New York, 1991) and *Tales of Power* (New York: Touchstone, 1972).

82. *The Shaman's Body*, vii–ix.

83. https://www.supanet.com/find/famous-quotes-by/eleonora-duse/if-the-sight-of-the-blue-fqb51886/

84. *ProcessMind: A User's Guide to Connecting with the Mind of God* (Quest Books, Wheaton, Ill., 2010).

85. I was amazed to find a strikingly similar story about the Mahalakshmi temple in Mumbai, India, which was built around 1785. In that story, a sea-wall was being constructed to protect Mumbai from flooding. However, the wall collapsed several times. The chief engineer, who was trying to build the wall, then dreamt of a statue of the Hindu goddess, Lakshmi, that was in the sea. In fact, a

statue of Lakshmi was found in the water, and the engineer then built a temple in the goddess's honor. After that, the construction of the wall was completed without any problems! These stories give us a sense of the power of the earth and its spirits to create reality! https://en.wikipedia.org/wiki/Hornby_Vellard and https://en.wikipedia.org/wiki/Mahalakshmi_Temple,_Mumbai

86. D. T. Suzuki, quoted in John Daido Loori's *The Zen of Creativity: Cultivating Your Artistic Life* (New York: Ballantine Books, 2005), 169.

87. The basic part of this exercise is adapted from the exercises found in Arny's book, *Processmind*.

88. https://sandra-silberzweig.pixels.com/

89. See some of the children's art from around the world on Silberzweig's facebook page: https://www.facebook.com/Silberzweig.Artwork/

90. I found the basic format of these directions on a great website—http://www.smallhandsbigart.com/silberzweig-self-portraits—which adapts some of Sandra Silberzweig's art and methods for children. I am so thankful to the teacher who experimented with this method, posting this, and some wonderful pictures of the portraits that her students made!

91. See his book, *Dance of the Ancient One.*

92. Wikipedia contributors. (2018, April 8). Hasegawa Tōhaku. In *Wikipedia, The Free Encyclopedia*. Retrieved 00:45, August 23, 2018, from https://en.wikipedia.org/w/index.php?title=Hasegawa_T%C5%8Dhaku&oldid=835460373

93. Some facilitators naturally use these noncognitive moments as a part or a central way of working. In con-

trast, many are frustrated by, or fearful of, noncognitive moments because they are afraid they will lose track of their skills and their linear orientation. However, if you are able to let go, *with* awareness, exploring noncognitive moments can often be the beginning of new insights and a deeper reconnection to the methods you have learned.

94. See Arny's *Dance of the Ancient One* (Portland, OR: Deep Democracy Exchange, 2012), 5, 27-28.

95. https://www.newyorker.com/culture/cultural-comment/a-transcendent-patti-smith-accepts-bob-dylans-nobel-prize , by Amanda Petrusich, December 10, 2016.

96. Ibid.

97. https://www.bobdylan.com/songs/hard-rains-gonna-fall/.

98. https://www.brainyquote.com/quotes/martha_graham_133358

99. http://www.art-quotes.com/auth_search.php?authid=5536#.XBC6nWhKg2w

100. See Arny's book, *The Leader's Second Training,* for much more about childhood dreams and memories as life patterns and gifts.

101. See Arny's *Coma: The Dreambody Near Death.* Portland, OR: Lao Tse Press, 2009. See also Alan Strachan's article *"The Wisdom of the Dreaming Body: On The Relationship Between Childhood Dreams And Adult Illnesses,"* http://alanstrachan.com/Dreaming_Childhood.html. I would also recommend Ioanna Velali's final project for her diploma in Process Work, *"Ways of Being": A Creative/Educational Project Exploring the Relationship between Life Myth and the Therapist's Style,* 2016 at http://www.processwork.org/

files/Finalprojects/Velali,_I_May_2016.pdf, where she approaches this theme and speaks about the facilitator's styles.

102. See my book *Alternative to Therapy*, 336–339, for an exercise to explore your first dream when you entered therapy or began to study psychology.

103. See his book, *The Leader's Second Training*.

104. Recently, I was very excited to find what I think may be Picasso's earliest childhood dream! He told one of his partners the following: "When I was a child, I often had a dream that used to frighten me greatly. I dreamed that my legs and arms grew to an enormous size and then shrank back just as much, in the other direction. And all around me, in my dream, I saw other people going through the same transformations, getting huge or very tiny. I felt terribly anguished every time I dreamed about that." Found in John Richardson, *A Life of Picasso: The Triumphant Years, 1917–1932.* (New York: Knopf, 2007), 35. This dream seems to illuminate a basic pattern behind many of his paintings; that is, the changing significance and proportions of different body parts, objects, and nature. So, if we assume this is his earliest dream, we can say that we don't know exactly what he will paint in a given moment, but his basic dream pattern is most often in the background of his art.

105. https://www.goodreads.com/quotes/tag/lailah-gifty-akita-affirmations?page=5

106. See my article, "Process Work and the Art of Animation" at https://static1.squarespace.com/static/54a386c7e4b079 85e3618194/t/557c5d44e4b0d0b21b858e14/14342137 00430/animation.pdf for more on this theme Also, see

Arny's *Quantum Mind,* 134–139, where he speaks about the steps and the dance in terms of calculus!

107. *Conflict: Phases, Forums, and Solutions* (Portland, OR: CreateSpace Independent Publishing Platform, 2017).

Made in the USA
Columbia, SC
20 February 2020

88189544R00163